Drew Provan

iPad

6th edition
covers all versions of iPad Mini and iPad 2 – iPad Air 2
with iOS 8

In easy steps is an imprint of In Easy Steps Limited
16 Hamilton Terrace · Holly Walk · Leamington Spa
Warwickshire · United Kingdom · CV32 4LY
www.ineasysteps.com

Sixth Edition

Notice of Liability
Every effort has been made to ensure that this book contains accurate
and current information. However, In Easy Steps Limited and the
author shall not be liable for any loss or damage suffered by readers
as a result of any information contained herein.

Trademarks
All trademarks are acknowledged as belonging to their respective
companies.

In Easy Steps Limited supports The Forest Stewardship Council (FSC),
the leading international forest certification organisation. All our titles
that are printed on Greenpeace approved FSC certified paper carry the
FSC logo.

MIX
Paper from
responsible sources
FSC® C020837

Printed and bound in the United Kingdom

ISBN 978-1-84078-636-1

Contents

1 Welcome to Your New iPad

The iPad is a multimedia tablet like no other. Its rich graphics and seamless integration with the preinstalled apps make it perfect for work and play. Most tasks requiring a laptop can be carried out on the iPad, (with its iOS 8 operating system) which is light, power-efficient, instantly-on and incredibly intuitive to use. It also has an huge number of third-party apps to expand its already impressive capabilities and performance.

Welcome to the iPad!

Congratulations on buying an iPad, a sophisticated multimedia tablet computer capable of playing music, dealing with emails, browsing the Web, organizing your calendar and thousands of other applications! Or maybe you haven't bought an iPad yet but are considering doing so. Let's look at what you can use the iPad for:

- Listening to music
- Recording and watching videos
- Taking photos
- Reading ebooks
- Browsing the Web
- Emails, contacts and calendars
- Social networking
- FaceTime video chats, playing games, and much more

Will it replace my laptop?

Probably not, although for many functions it can be used instead of a laptop. It depends on what you use your laptop for. If you mainly do web browsing, check emails and use social networking apps then the iPad can easily replace your laptop. If, on the other hand, you use your laptop to generate PowerPoint slides or create complex documents then the iPad may not be ideal, since some functions are missing from the iPad.

What's missing from the iPad?

There are features found on laptops and desktops that are missing from the iPad. At present there is no:

- SD card slot.
- USB slots (though the Apple Camera Kit does have a 30-pin plug which has a USB socket at one end, but this is to connect your camera rather than attach other devices).
- The ability to access files and drag them around or drop into folders is not available on the iPad. You can get files on there but it's clunky and not very intuitive.

Depending on your needs, the iPad may not be a laptop replacement. Assess your needs carefully before buying one!

Apple's website (www. apple.com) has Q and As and lots of helpful tips on using the iPad.

The New icon pictured above indicates a new or enhanced feature introduced on the iPad with the latest version iOS 8.

iPad Specifications

Since its introduction there are now several different generations of iPad, including the iPad Mini, which is smaller than the original iPad. When considering which iPad is best for you, some of the specifications to consider are:

- **Processor:** This determines the speed at which the iPad operates and how quickly tasks are performed.

- **Storage:** This determines how much content you can store on your iPad. Across the iPad family, the range of storage is 16GB, 32GB, 64GB or 128GB.

- **Connectivity:** The options for this are Wi-Fi and 3G/4G connectivity for the Internet and Bluetooth for connecting to other devices over short distances. All models of iPad have Wi-Fi connectivity as standard.

- **Screen:** Look for an iPad with a Retina Display screen for the highest resolution and best clarity. This is an LED-backlit screen and is available on the latest iPads, the iPad Air 2 and the iPad Mini 3.

- **Operating System**: The full size version of the iPad and the iPad Mini both run on the iOS 8 operating system.

- **Battery power:** This is the length of time the iPad can be used for general use such as surfing the Web on Wi-Fi, watching video, or listening to music. All models offer approximately 10 hours of use in this way.

- **Input/Output:** Both the iPad and the iPad Mini have similar output/input options. These are a Lightning connector port (for charging), 3.5 mm stereo headphone minijack, built-in speaker, microphone and micro-SIM card tray (Wi-Fi and 4G model only).

- **Sensors:** These are used to access the amount of ambient light and also the orientation in which the iPad is being held. The sensors include an accelerometer, ambient light sensor and gyroscope.

- **TV and video:** This determines how your iPad can be connected to a High Definition TV. This is done with AirPlay Mirroring, which lets you send what's on your iPad screen to an HDTV wirelessly with AppleTV.

The latest versions of the iPad family, released in October 2014, are the iPad Air 2 for the full size version (sixth generation) and the iPad Mini 3.

If you have a fourth generation iPad (or later) then it'll come with the new Lightning connector. You'll need to buy adapters to connect it to your "old" 30-pin accessories, such as TV, iPod dock, etc.

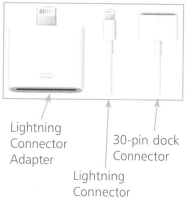

Lightning Connector Adapter

30-pin dock Connector

Lightning Connector

What's New in iOS 8?

iOS 8 is the latest version of the operating system for Apple's mobile devices including the iPad, the iPhone and the iPod Touch.

iOS 8 is an evolution of iOS 7, which was one of the most dramatic cosmetic changes to the operating system in its history. It produced a flatter, cleaner, design and this has been continued with iOS 8, which is not greatly different in appearance to its predecessor.

Linking it all up

One of the features of iOS 8 is the way it links up with other Apple devices, whether it is something like an iPhone also using iOS 8, or an Apple desktop or laptop computer running the OS X Yosemite operating system. This works with apps such as Mail and Photos, so you can start an email on one device and finish it on another, or take a photo on one device and have it available on all other compatible Apple devices. Most of this is done through iCloud and once it is set up it takes care of most of these tasks automatically. (See Chapter Two (pages 40-50) for details about setting up and using iCloud, Family Sharing and iCloud Drive.)

iOS 8 can be used on all iPads from the iPad 2 upwards and all versions of the iPad Mini.

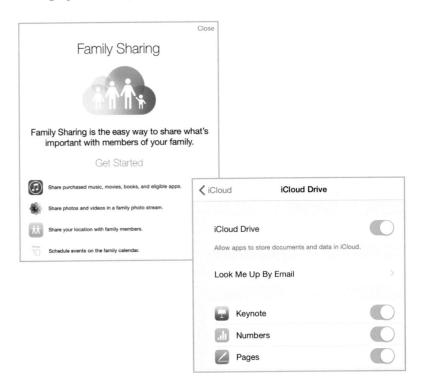

New and improved apps

Several of the iOS 8 apps have been updated and improved: the Messages app now enables group texts, video messages and displaying your locations; the Photos app has increased sharing capabilities; the Camera app now has a time lapse option; and the keyboard has an option for using predictive text.

There is also a new Tips app and the iBooks and Podcasts apps are now preinstalled, saving the need to download them from the App Store.

Check back for new tips every week.

The iBooks and Podcasts apps are sometimes grouped in a folder named Extras.

iOS 8 is an operating system that is stylish and versatile on the iPad and it also plays an important role in the holy grail of computing: linking desktop and mobile devices so that users can spend more time doing the things that matter to them, safe in the knowledge that their content will be backed up and available across multiple devices.

iOS 8 on the iPad does not contain the Health app, which is available with iOS 8 on the iPhone.

Finding Your Way Around

The physical buttons and controls on the iPad are very simple. Additional functions such as screen brightness are software-controlled.

Don't forget

When you first unpack your iPad you will also find a Lightning/USB cable for charging the iPad or connecting it to a computer. There will also be a USB power adapter for charging the iPad. There is a range of iPad accessories available from the Apple Store, one of the most useful being a Smart Cover, for protecting the iPad and also putting it to sleep when not in use.

14

Status bar · FaceTime camera · Sleep/Wake/On/Off

Micro-SIM tray (some models)

App icons

Home button

Don't forget

The iPad Air 2 does not have a side switch, but all other models of the iPad and iPad Mini do. For models with a side switch, this can be used to mute the sound on the iPad, or lock rotation of the screen (see page 72).

iSight Camera · Microphone · Headset Jack

Side switch

Side switch

Volume Up/ Down

Volume

iPad

Speaker · Lightning connector

The **network data icons** at the top of the screen are pretty much like those found on the iPhone.

iPad ᦓ		14:13	⚡ 36% 🔋
Settings		**Bluetooth**	
✈ Airplane Mode ⬤		Bluetooth	⬤
ᦓ Wi-Fi NETGEAR		DEVICES	
✳ Bluetooth On		Searching…	

The fastest data connection is Wi-Fi. If no Wi-Fi is available you will need to use 3G/4G (if your iPad has this option) which is fairly fast. Unfortunately, as you move around, the 3G/4G signal will come and go so you may see the 3G/4G disappear and be replaced by the EDGE symbol (E). EDGE is slower than 3G/4G.

If you're *really* unlucky, the EDGE signal may vanish and you may see the GPRS symbol. GPRS is *very* slow!

o	GPRS (slowest)	➤	Location services
E	EDGE	🔒	Lock
3G	3G	**LTE**	LTE
4G	4G	➿	Personal Hotspot
📶	Wi-Fi	▶	Play
✳	Bluetooth	🔄	Screen lock
✈	Airplane mode	🔄	Syncing
✳	iPad is busy		

The GPRS, EDGE and 3G/4G icons are seen on the Wi-Fi and cellular models only.

Don't forget

The iPad has many features which make it accessible to those with specific visual and audio needs. These features are covered in detail on pages 230-234.

Home Button and Screen

There are very few actual physical buttons on the iPad but the Home button is an important one. The Home button functions changed since the arrival of iOS 4.2, allowing you to see active apps in the Multitasking bar.

You can quit active multitasking apps (this was not possible with earlier versions of iPad).

- If you are on the Home screen (the first screen) press and hold the Home button to activate the Siri voice search assistant function.

- If you are on any other screen press the Home button to go back to the Home screen: this saves you having to flick the screens to the left.

- When using the Music app with Home button it minimizes the Music window, allowing you to use other apps while listening to music.

- Pressing the Home button quickly twice brings up the Multitasking window (shows your active apps).

You can see your active apps by bringing up the Multitasking window. If an app is misbehaving, quit it using the Multitasking window.

16

To see the Multitasking window without having to press the Home Button twice, drag four fingers up the screen. You can also drag four fingers right or left across the screen to switch between open apps.

The **Home screen** is the first screen you see when you start up the iPad. It contains the apps installed by Apple (and these cannot be deleted). In all, there are 20 of these – four will be on the Dock.

The Dock comes with four apps attached. You can move these off, add other apps (the Dock can hold a maximum of six apps or folders), or you can put your favorite apps there and remove those placed on the Dock by Apple.

You can move these apps to other screens if you want to but it's a good idea to keep the most important or most frequently-used apps on this screen.

The iBooks and Podcasts apps are now preinstalled on the iPad: in previous versions of iOS they had to be downloaded separately, from the App Store.

Hot tip

By default there are four apps on the Dock at the bottom of the screen. You can add two more if needed.

You can even drag folders to the Dock.

Don't forget

To move an app, press and hold on it until it starts to jiggle. Then, drag it into a new position or onto the Dock. To move an app to another screen, press and hold on it and move it to the edge of the screen, until the next screen appears.

Network connections   Time   Battery

Wallpaper

Preinstalled apps   iPad screens   Apps on the Dock (up to 6)

Multitasking Window

The iPad can run several programs at once and these can be managed by the Multitasking window. This has been redesigned for iOS 8 and it performs a number of tasks:

- It shows open apps

- It enables you to move between open apps and open different ones

- It enables apps to be closed (see next page)

Accessing Multitasking

The Multitasking option can be accessed from any screen on your iPad, as follows:

 Double-click on the **Home** button

2 The currently-open apps are displayed, with their icons underneath them (except the Home screen). The most recently-used apps are shown first. At the top of the Multitasking window are the people with whom you have most recently been in contact via email or Messages

3 Swipe left and right to view the open apps. Tap on one to access it in full screen size

Tap on one of the recent contacts at the top of the Multitasking window to send them an email or an iMessage.

Closing Items

The iPad deals with open apps very efficiently. They do not interact with other apps, which increases security and also means that they can be open in the background, without using up a significant amount of processing power, in a state of semi-hibernation until they are needed. Because of this it is not essential to close apps when you move to something else. However, you may want to close apps if you feel you have too many open or if one stops working. To do this:

1 Access the Multitasking window. The currently-open apps are displayed

2 Press and hold on an app and swipe it to the top of the screen to close it. This does not remove it from the iPad and it can be opened again in the usual way

3 The app is removed from its position in the Multitasking window

Don't forget

When you switch from one app to another, the first one stays open in the background. You can go back to it by accessing it from the Multitasking window or the Home screen.

In the Control Center

The Control Center is a panel containing some of the most commonly used options within the **Settings** app. It can be accessed with one swipe and is an excellent function for when you do not want to have to go into Settings.

Accessing the Control Center

The Control Center can be accessed from any screen within iOS 8 and it can also be accessed from the Lock Screen:

 Tap on the **Settings** app

Beware

The Control Center cannot be disabled from being accessed from the Home screen.

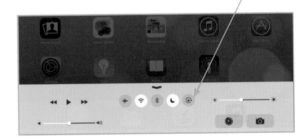 Tap on the **Control Center** tab and drag the **Access on Lock Screen** and **Access Within Apps** buttons On or Off to specify if the Control Center can be accessed from there (if both are Off, it can still be accessed from any Home screen)

 Swipe up from the bottom of any screen to access the Control Center panel

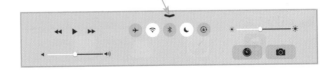

 Tap on this button to hide the Control Center panel, or tap anywhere on the screen

Control Center controls

The items that can be used in the Control Center are:

1 Use these controls for any music or video that is playing. Use the buttons to Pause/Play a track, go to the beginning or end and drag the slider to adjust the volume

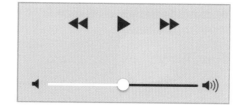

2 Tap on this button to turn **Airplane mode** On or Off

3 Tap on this button to turn **Wi-Fi** On or Off

4 Tap on this button to turn **Bluetooth** On or Off

5 Tap on this button to turn **Do Not Disturb** mode On or Off

6 Tap on this button to access a clock, including a stopwatch

7 Tap on this button to open the **Camera** app

8 Use this slider to adjust the screen brightness

9 Tap on this button to **Lock** or **Unlock** screen rotation. If it is locked, the screen will not change when you change the orientation of your iPad

21

Hot tip

The screen rotation can also be locked from within the **General** section of the **Settings** app. Under **Use Side Switch to**, tap on the **Lock Rotation** link. Then the side switch can be used to lock, and unlock, the screen rotation. The iPad Air 2 does not have a side switch, but all other models do.

Finding Things on the iPad

Sometimes you haven't got time to look through your entire calendar for an appointment, or to scroll through iTunes for one track. You can use Spotlight (Apple's indexing and search facility) to find specific apps, contacts, emails, appointments and music content.

Start search

Hot tip

Search using Spotlight to avoid spending ages looking for emails, music tracks and other data.

1 From any free area on a Home screen, press and hold and swipe downwards

2 You will be taken to the Spotlight search screen

3 Enter your search word or string into the search box

4 Your results will show up below. The results are grouped according to their type, i.e. Calendar appointment, email, etc.

Finding Things with Siri

Siri is the iPad voice assistant that provides answers to a variety of questions by looking at your iPad and also web services. You can ask Siri questions relating to the apps on your iPad and also general questions, such as weather conditions around the world, or sports results. To set up:

 Open **Settings > General**, tap on the **Siri** link

 Drag the **Siri** button to **On** to activate the Siri functionality

Questioning Siri

Once you have set up Siri, you can start putting it to work with your queries. To do this:

 Hold down the **Home** button until the Siri window appears

What can I help you with?

Within the Siri Settings you can select a language and a voice style.

If you do not ask anything initially, Siri will prompt you with some suggestions (or tap on the **?** button in the bottom left-hand corner for more suggestions)

Some things you can ask me:

What's my ETA?

Tweet great show last night

Search Twitter for SF Giants

Play Norah Jones

Check my email

 Tap on the microphone button to ask a question of Siri

Default Applications

These are the preinstalled apps:

With iOS 8 the iBooks and Podcasts apps are now included as preinstalled apps: in previous versions they had to be downloaded separately from the App Store. There is also a Tips app which provides help and advice about different features and apps within iOS 8.

iBooks

Podcasts

Tips

 Calendar: keeps your appointments in sync with your PC or Mac using wired or wireless sync

Contacts: list of all contacts including phone numbers, email, postal addresses and notes

Notes: for jotting things down. Sync with your computer or you can email them to yourself

 Maps: GPS-enabled maps help you get from A to B, current position, and other information

 Videos: play movies and other video content, purchased or from your own collection

iTunes Store: browse and buy music, movies, TV shows and more

App Store: your central store for paid and free apps

 Reminders: to-do lists, sync with Apple Mail and Outlook Tasks

 Messages: send SMS-type messages free with Wi-Fi

Settings: this is where you make changes to personalize your iPad

 Safari: Apple's home-grown web browser

 Mail: handles IMAP and POP3 email, and syncs to your main accounts on your computer

 Photos: show your photos with slideshows, print off photos or share via Facebook, Twitter, etc.

 Music: controls music, podcasts, etc.

 Game Center: social gaming, lets you play games and interact with friends

 Camera: shoot stills or movies using front or back cameras similar to iPhone functionality

 FaceTime: video chat to others using iPad, iPhone 4 and 5 or Mac

 Photo Booth: take still images and select from a series of special effects

 Newsstand: stores your newspaper and magazine subscriptions

 Clock: provides time in any part of the world. Useful as an alarm clock and a stopwatch

The Display and Keyboard

What's all the excitement about the screen? What makes it so special? Firstly, it is a high quality Retina Display.

The technology behind the multi-touch screen is ingenious. Using one, two, three or four fingers you can do lots of different things on the iPad depending on the app you're using and what you want to do. The main actions are tap, flick, pinch/spread and drag.

The screen is designed to be used with fingers – the skin on glass contact is required (if you tap using your nail you will find it won't work). There are styluses you can buy for the iPad but for full functionality, fingers on screen give the best results.

Beware

The screen responds best to skin contact. Avoid using pens or other items to tap the screen.

Tap	Apps open when you tap their icons. Within apps you can select photos, music, web links and many other functions. The tap is similar to a single click with a mouse on the computer
Flick	You can flick through lists like Contacts, Songs, or anywhere there's a long list. Place your finger on the screen and quickly flick up and down and the list scrolls rapidly up and down
Pinch/spread	The iPad screen responds to two fingers placed on its surface. To reduce the size of a photo or web page in Safari place two fingers on the screen and bring them together. To enlarge the image or web page spread your fingers apart and the image grows in size
Drag	You can drag web pages and maps around if you are unable to see the edges. Simply place your finger on the screen and keep it there but move the image or web page around until you can see the hidden areas

Hot tip

Use four fingers to bring up the Multitasking window (drag four fingers up the screen), or flick right or left using four fingers to switch between running apps.

...cont'd

The iPad is different to a laptop since there is no physical keyboard. Instead, you type by tapping the **virtual keyboard** on the iPad screen itself. You can use the keyboard in portrait or landscape modes. The landscape version provides much wider keys.

The keyboard seems to change in different apps

The keyboard is smart – and should match the app you're in. For example, if you are word processing or entering regular text you will see a standard keyboard. But if you are using a browser or are prompted to enter an email address you will see a modified keyboard with *.com* and @ symbols prominently displayed.

Hot tip

If you have Wi-Fi, try using your voice to dictate emails and other text using the Dictate option (its icon is on the left of the spacebar).

Top left: portrait keyboard in Mail.

Top right: portrait keyboard in Pages.

Bottom left: portrait keyboard in Safari – note the **Return** key has now changed to **Go**. Tap this to search the web or go to a specific URL.

If you find you are making lots of typing errors, try switching the iPad to landscape mode (keys are larger).

Mail with iPad in the landscape position. Notice how wide the keys have become, making it easier to type without hitting two keys at once! Also notice the Dictation icon to the left of the spacebar (you get this when on Wi-Fi).

The keyboard in the Apple productivity apps, Pages, Keynote and Numbers, still uses the old-style keyboard, which has the same functionality but has gray keys instead of white ones.

Pages with landscape keyboard. Again, the keyboard is large but the downside is that you lose real estate for work – the effective area for viewing content is quite small. Dictation is active – you can tell because the icon has enlarged and shows the volume level as you dictate your text.

Caps Lock and Auto-Correct

It's annoying when you want to type something entirely in upper case letters since you have to press Shift for every letter – or do you? Actually, there's a setting which will activate Caps Lock but you need to activate this in settings:

● Go to **Settings**

● Select **General**

● Select **Keyboard**

● Make sure the **Enable Caps Lock** slider is set to **On**

● While you are there, make sure the other settings are on, for example "**.**" **Shortcut** – this helps you add a period by tapping the spacebar twice (much like the BlackBerry)

Hot tip

If you do not like the default iPad keyboard you can download other third-party virtual ones from the App Store. Three to look at are, SwiftKey, Swype and KuaiBoard.

iPad ⬢		17:18		Not Charging
Settings		‹ General	Keyboards	
✈ Airplane Mode	⬤			
⬢ Wi-Fi	PlusnetWireless792287	Keyboards		2 ›
⬢ Bluetooth	Off	Hardware Keyboard		›
⬢ Notifications		Shortcuts		›
⬢ Control Center				
⬢ Do Not Disturb		Auto-Capitalization		⬤
		Auto-Correction		⬤
		Check Spelling		⬤
⬢ General		Enable Caps Lock		⬤
⬢ Display & Brightness		Predictive		◯
⬢ Wallpaper		Split Keyboard		⬤
⬢ Sounds		"." Shortcut		⬤
⬢ Passcode		Double tapping the space bar will insert a period followed by a space.		

Other settings for the keyboard

● **Auto-Correction** suggests the correct word. If it annoys you, switch it off

● **Auto-Capitalization** is great for putting capitals in names

● The "**.**" **Shortcut** types a period every time you hit the spacebar twice. This saves time when typing long emails but if you prefer not to use this, switch it off. Here's another neat trick – you can also insert a period by tapping the spacebar with two fingers simultaneously

...cont'd

As you type words, the iPad **Auto-Correct** will suggest words intelligently which will speed up your typing.

To accept iPad suggestion

When the suggested word pops up, simply tap the space bar and it will be inserted. The suggested word may not be what you want, in which case you can reject it by tapping the 'x'.

To reject suggestion

Above left: iPad will suggest a word but if you don't want to use the suggestion tap the 'x'. The word you type will be added to your user dictionary. Above right: You can look up the dictionary: tap word twice, tap the right arrow and choose Define.

All contact names are automatically added to your user dictionary.

Can I Use a Real Keyboard?

There are times when you need real physical keys, for example if you are typing a longer document you might find tapping out your text on the glass screen annoying. Apple has designed a dock with an integrated keyboard, which is great for holding your iPad at the correct angle, and allowing your iPad to be charged while you type using the keyboard.

For some older keyboards you will need the Lightning to 30-pin Adapter.

Original Apple iPad Keyboard and dock

ZAGGmate keyboard for iPad 2 (works with later models too)

If you need to type long documents consider using a physical keyboard.

Can I use a Bluetooth keyboard?

Absolutely! The iPad has Bluetooth built-in so you can hook up an Apple Bluetooth keyboard and type away. Alternatively, there are third-party keyboards such as the ZAGGmate Bluetooth keyboard (**www.zagg.com**) which acts as a case when not in use (protects the front of the iPad but not the back).

Keyboard Tricks

Although it's not immediately obvious, the keyboard can generate accents, acutes, and many other foreign characters and symbols.

Holding the letter "u" or "e" generates lots of variants. Just slide your finger along till you reach the one you want and it will be inserted into the document.

For accents and other additional characters, touch the key then slide your finger to the character you want to use.

Also, when you use Safari you don't have to enter ".co.uk" in URLs – the **?** key will produce other endings if you touch and hold the key.

Select, Copy and Paste Text

Rather than retype text, you can select text (or pictures) and paste these into other documents or the URL field in Safari. Touch and hold text, images or URL (links) to open, save or copy them.

To select text

Touch and hold a paragraph of text to select. Drag the blue handles to enclose the text you want to copy then tap **Copy**.

Copy web links by tapping and selecting **Copy**. If you just want to go to the site, click **Open in New Tab**.

Paste copied text or images by tapping screen in Pages, for example.

Use the built-in dictionary by tapping a word then Define.

Making Corrections

Sometimes words get mistyped. You could retype the whole word but it's easier to correct. Since the iPad isn't a laptop there is no mouse and pointer so you need to get the cursor next to the incorrect character. You can then delete that character and replace it with the correct character.

To position the cursor where you want it

1 Put your finger onto the incorrect word (you may need to tap and hold)

2 Keep your finger on the screen and slide your finger along the word until the cursor is just ahead of the incorrect letter(s)

3 Backspace (delete from right to left) and delete the incorrect character(s)

4 Insert the correct character(s) then locate the end of your text and tap the screen to position the cursor at the end so you can start typing again

5 The iPad can help you if you don't know how to spell the word (tap **Replace...** and it will suggest some words)

Hot tip

You can also correct by double-tapping the incorrectly-spelled word and choosing **Replace** then selecting the correct word.

Using Predictive Text

Predictive text tries to guess what you are typing and also predict the next word following the one you have just typed. It was developed primarily for text messaging and it has now been introduced to the iPad with iOS 8. To use it:

1 Tap on the **General** tab in the Settings app

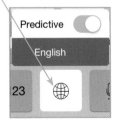
2 Tap on the **Keyboard** link

3 Drag the **Predictive** button **On**

4 When predictive text is activated the QuickType bar is displayed above the keyboard. Initially this has a suggestion for the first work to include. Tap on a word or start typing

5 As you type, suggestions appear. Tap on one to accept it. Tap on the word within the quotation marks to accept exactly what you have typed

6 After you have typed a word a suggestion for the next word appears. Tap on it to use it, or ignore it if you wish.

2 Getting Started

As with most technology, although the iPad is plug-and-play, there is some initial setting up to do. It's worth spending some time setting up the iPad so it best suits your needs.

Turn On and Register

You can put your iPad fully off or into sleep mode (sleep mode is useful because as soon as you press the Home button the iPad is instantly on).

- If the iPad is fully off, press and hold the **On/Off** button – the iPad will boot up

- When you have finished using it simply press the **On/Off** button briefly and the iPad will enter sleep mode again

- Sleep mode uses very little power so for the sake of speed simply use sleep mode unless you are not going to use the iPad for several days

- To wake from sleep, press the **Home button** or **On/Off** switch

To fully power off

1 Press and hold the **On/Off** button until you see the slider bar and **Slide to Power Off** appears

2 Slide the red slider to the right

3 The iPad will fully shut down

Lock the screen

The iPad works in portrait (upright) and landscape (sideways) modes. The iPad is clever and can tell which way up it is being held and the screen will rotate accordingly. Sometimes you will want it to stay fixed in portrait or landscape modes. This can be done with the Screen Lock function. This can be controlled by the Control Center. To do this, swipe up from the bottom of the screen and tap on this button.

Hot tip

You can configure the Side Switch to lock the screen in portrait or landscape mode by choosing **General settings > Use Side Switch to: Lock Rotation or Mute**.

...cont'd

Like the iPhone, the iPad needs to be **registered** with Apple before you can use it.

To register

Plug the iPad into your computer (Mac or PC) using the sync cable provided and iTunes should open automatically. If not, double-click app to **launch iTunes** manually

The Devices tab on the right side of the iTunes window should show the **iPad**. You will then see the **Welcome to Your New iPad** pane in iTunes

Click **Continue** to reach the next screen

Accept the license conditions and click **Continue**

The next pane requests your iTunes account ID and password. If you do not have an iTunes account click the **I do not have an Apple ID** option. Click **Continue**

The next page will ask if you want to use iCloud for Push Email/Calendar and Contacts

Either choose to use your existing iCloud account, or register for one, or if you don't want iCloud select **Not Now**

The next pane lets you **Name** your iPad and decide how you want to sync your data (songs, videos, and other content) to the iPad

If you want songs and videos to sync automatically check the boxes marked **Automatically Sync Songs and Videos to My iPad**, **Automatically Add Photos to my iPad**, and **Automatically Sync Applications to my iPad**

iTunes is the Apple music and media player and also has access to the online iTunes Store. It is preinstalled on Mac computers, but if you need to download it for a PC, this has to be done from the Apple website and click on the iTunes tab on the top toolbar.

You can register your iPad directly from the iPad too. You will need to be online (see page 51). Go to **Settings > iTunes & App Store.** Tap **Create Apple ID** and follow the instructions that appear on your iPad. However, it is a good idea to plug the iPad into your Mac or PC regularly so you have a recent backup of all your files, music, and apps. If you activate iCloud, all of the items you select will automatically be backed up to the iCloud when you are connected to the Internet via Wi-Fi.

Syncing with iTunes

The iPad and iOS 8 are both very much linked to the online world and the iCloud service can be used to store and synchronize several types of content. However, it is still possible to use iTunes on a Mac or PC to sync content, including:

- Music

- Videos

- Apps

- TV shows

- Podcast

- Books

iTunes can be used so that you can sync these items (or some of them) onto your iPad. To do this:

Don't forget

In some previous version of iOS, other types of content could be synced with iTunes, such as Notes and Calendars. However, these can now all be saved, stored and synced in iCloud. See the pages 40-45 for more detailed information about iCloud.

1 Connect your iPad to your computer. iTunes should open automatically but if it does not, launch it in the usual way. Click on your iPad at the top left-hand corner of the iTunes window. Click on the **Summary** tab to view general details about your iPad

 iTunes can also be used to back up your iPad (in addition to iCloud). To do this, click on the **This computer** button under the **Automatically Back Up** section or click on the **Back Up Now** button

3 Click on the tabs in the left-hand panel to select the items that you want to sync. These include Apps, Music, Movies, TV Shows, Podcasts, Audiobooks, Books and Photos

4 Select what you want to sync for each heading (such as selected music and playlists, or your entire library)

When you are syncing items to your iPad it is best to select specific folders or files, rather than including everything. This is because items such as music, videos and photos can take up a lot of storage space on your iPad if you sync a large library from your computer.

39

5 Click on the **Apply** button to start the sync process and copy the selected items to your iPad

6 On the **Summary** page, scroll down to view the options for syncing, such as specifying only checked songs and videos to be synced, or

Options

- ☑ Open iTunes when this iPad is connected
- ☐ Sync with this iPad over Wi-Fi
- ☑ Sync only checked songs and videos
- ☐ Prefer standard definition videos
- ☐ Convert higher bit rate songs to 128 kbps ○ AAC
- ☐ Manually manage music and videos
- Reset Warnings
- Configure Accessibility...

manually manage your music and videos for syncing

Using iCloud

iCloud is a service that allows you to use the cloud to sync your data (calendars, contacts, mail, Safari bookmarks, and notes) wirelessly.

Once you are registered and set up, any entries or deletions to calendars and other apps are reflected in all devices using iCloud.

An Apple ID is required for using iCloud, and this can be obtained online at **https://appleid.apple.com/** or you can create an Apple ID when you first access an app on your iPad that requires this for use. It is free to create an Apple ID and requires a username and password. Once you have created an Apple ID you can then use the full range of iCloud services.

iCloud settings

Once you have set up your iCloud account you can then apply settings for how it works. Once you have done this you will not have to worry about it again:

The iPad apps that require an Apple ID to access their full functionality include: iTunes Store, iMessages, iBooks, FaceTime and the App Store.

1 Access the **iCloud** section in the Settings app

2 Drag these buttons to On for each item that you wish to be included in iCloud. Each item is then saved and stored in the iCloud and made available to your other iCloud-enabled devices

Using iCloud online

Once you have created an Apple ID you will automatically have an iCloud account. This can be used to sync your data from your iPad and you can also access your content online from the iCloud website at **www.icloud.com**

 Enter your Apple ID details

 The full range of iCloud apps is displayed, including those for Pages, Numbers and Keynote

3 Click on an app to view its details. If iCloud is set up on your iPad, any changes made here will be displayed in the online app too

Find my iPad

This is a great feature which allows you to see where your devices are. Once activated (**Settings > iCloud > Find My iPad**), log into iCloud using a browser and click Find My iPhone. This will find your iPad and any other devices you have registered.

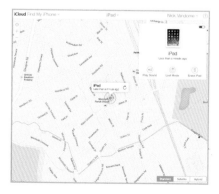

iCloud provides 5GB free storage but you can pay for more. (*Correct at the time of printing.*) For example, I upgraded my iCloud storage to 25GB.

About the iCloud Drive

One of the options in the iCloud section is for the Cloud Drive. This can be used to store documents so that you can use them on any other Apple devices that you have, such as an iPhone or a MacBook. To set up iCloud Drive:

 In the iCloud section of the Settings app, tap on the **iCloud Drive** button

🌥 iCloud Drive	Off ⟩

 Tap on the **iCloud Drive** button so that it is **On**

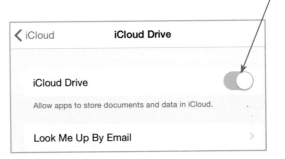

⟨ iCloud **iCloud Drive**

iCloud Drive

Allow apps to store documents and data in iCloud.

Look Me Up By Email ⟩

 Once iCloud Drive has been activated, tap on any listed apps so that they can use iCloud Drive

⟨ iCloud **iCloud Drive**

iCloud Drive

Allow apps to store documents and data in iCloud.

Look Me Up By Email ⟩

📊 Keynote

📊 Numbers

📝 Pages

🧭 Safari

4 When you are using an app that has iCloud Drive capabilities it may ask you to turn on iCloud Drive for the specific app, if it has not already been done. Tap on the **OK** button and open the Settings app

5 In the Settings app, open the settings for the specific app (in this case, Pages) and drag the **Use iCloud** button to **On**. Any document created, or edited, by this app will automatically be stored in the iCloud Drive

Pages
IPAD SETTINGS
Notifications >
PAGES SETTINGS
ICLOUD
Use iCloud

6 The documents in the app on your iPad can be viewed on your other Apple devices if you have iCloud turned on and iCloud Drive activated. For iOS 8 devices they can be viewed from the Documents section of the compatible apps (such as Pages, Numbers and Keynote); for OS X Yosemite devices they can be viewed in the iCloud Drive section in the Finder

Using iCloud Drive Online

Files that have been saved to your iCloud Drive on your iPad can also be accessed on any other Apple devices you have, such as an iPhone or a MacBook. They can also be accessed from your online iCloud account at **www.icloud.com**, from any Internet-enabled computer. To do this:

 Log in to your iCloud account and click on the iCloud Drive button on the Homepage

 Your iCloud Drive folders are displayed. Click on a folder to view its contents

3 Content created with the relevant apps on your iPad will automatically be stored in the appropriate folders, i.e. Pages documents in the Pages folder, etc.

Within a folder, use the buttons at the top of the window to, from left to right, create a new folder, upload a file from your computer, download a selected item from the iCloud Drive to your computer, or delete a selected item

5 From the Homepage of the online iCloud website, select one of the apps that use iCloud Drive, e.g. Pages, Numbers or Keynote

6 Create a document with the appropriate app. This will then be available on your iPad, using the equivalent app on your iPad

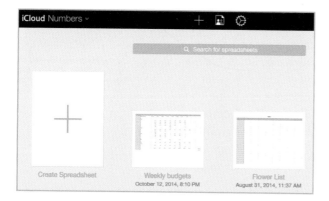

About Family Sharing

As everyone gets more and more digital devices it is becoming increasingly important to be able to share content with other people, particularly family members. In iOS 8, the Family Sharing function enables you to share items that you have downloaded from the App Store, such as music and movies, with up to six other family members, as long as they have an Apple Account. Once this has been set up it is also possible to share items such as family calendars, photos and even see where family members are within Maps. To set up and start using Family Sharing:

 Access the iCloud section within the Settings app, as shown on the previous pages

 Tap on the **Set Up Family Sharing** button

 Tap on the **Get Started** button

4 One person will be the organizer of Family Sharing, i.e. in charge of it, and if you set it up then it will be you. Tap on the **Continue** button (the Family Sharing account will then be linked to your Apple ID)

5 Tap on the **Continue** button again

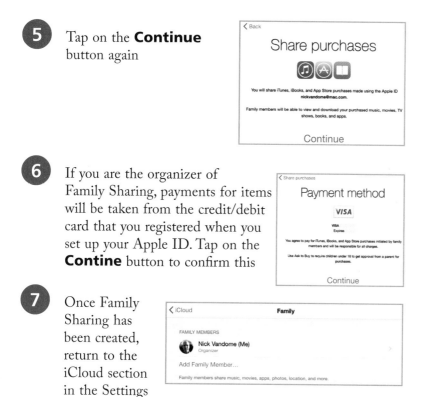

6 If you are the organizer of Family Sharing, payments for items will be taken from the credit/debit card that you registered when you set up your Apple ID. Tap on the **Contine** button to confirm this

7 Once Family Sharing has been created, return to the iCloud section in the Settings app and tap on the **Add Family Member** button

8 Enter the name or email address of a family member and tap on the **Next** button

9 An invitation is sent to the selected person. They have to accept this before they can participate in Family Sharing

Using Family Sharing

Once you have set up Family Sharing and added family members you can start sharing a selection of items.

Sharing Photos

Photos can be shared with Family Sharing thanks to the Family album that is created automatically within the Photos app, in the Shared section. To use this:

1 Tap on the **Photos** app

2 Tap the **Shared** button

3 The **Family** album is already available in the **Shared** section. Tap on the cloud button to access the album and start adding photos to it

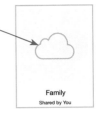

Family
Shared by You

4 Tap on this button to add photos to the album

< Sharing

+

5 Tap on the photos you want to add and tap on the **Done** button

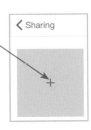

Done
Select

Hot tip

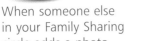

When someone else in your Family Sharing circle adds a photo to the Family album, you are notified in the Notification Center and also by a red notification on the Photos app.

6 Make sure the **Family** album is selected as the Shared Album and tap on the **Post** button

Cancel   iCloud   Post

3 Photos

Shared Album   Family

Sharing Calendars

Family Sharing also generates a Family calendar that can be used by all Family Sharing members:

1 Tap on the **Calendar** app

2 Tap the **Calendars** button to view the Family calendar

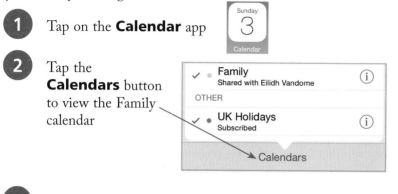

3 Press and hold on a date to create a New Event. The current calendar will probably not be the Family one. Tap on the calendar to change it

Calendar	• Home >

For a more on calendars and creating events, see Chapter Nine.

4 Tap on the **Family** calendar

- Work
- Birthdays
- Family
  Shared with Eilidh Vandome ✓

5 The **Family** calendar is now the active one

Calendar	• Family >

6 Complete the details for the event. It will be added to your calendar, with the Family tag. Other people in your Family Sharing circle will have this event added to their Family calendar too and they will be sent a notification

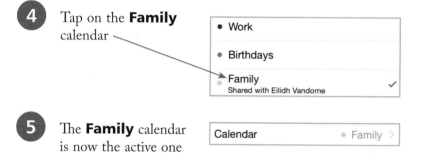

...cont'd

Sharing Music, Movies and Books

Family Sharing can be used to share items such as apps, music, movies and books between members of the group. This can be done on mobile devices or desktop or laptop Apple computers. To share items from another Family Sharing member:

 Open the **iTunes Store** app (or the **iBooks** app of the **App Store** app)

 Tap on the **Purchased** button

Purchased

3 Tap on the iCloud icon next to an item to download it to your own device

Songs	
Space Oddity David Bowie	
Ziggy Stardust David Bowie	
The Jean Genie David Bowie	

Sharing Locations

Family Sharing makes it easy to keep in touch with the rest of the family and see exactly where they are. This can be done with the Find My Friends app. The other person has to have their iPad (or other Apple device) turned on and online. To find family members:

1 Open the **App Store** app and download the **Find My Friends** app

Find My Friends
Apple
Essentials
FREE

2 A map is displayed with the location of any active and online members of the Family Sharing group

Beware

Family Sharing can be set up so that individuals have to gain permission from the sharing administrator to buy their own items from the App Store or iTunes Store. This is usually for children when they do not have a credit card registered with their iCloud account.

Hot tip

The Find My iPad app can be used in a similar way to Find My Friends and it can be used to find any lost or stolen devices belonging to members of the Family Sharing group.

Getting the iPad Online

The iPad is a fun device for listening to music, watching videos and playing games, but to experience the full potential you need to get it online.

Getting online
The fastest connection is Wi-Fi. All iPad models include the Wi-Fi receiver which means you can browse available wireless networks, choose one and connect.

1 Select **Settings > Wi-Fi**

2 Slide the Wi-Fi slider to **On** if it is **Off**

3 A list of available wireless networks will appear under **Choose a Network.** Tap the one you want to connect to

For a more detailed look at connecting with Wi-Fi see pages 67-68 in Chapter Three.

4 You will likely be prompted for a username and password since most networks are locked (if the network is *open* you will get straight on)

5 Check the signal strength indicator which will give you an idea of how strong the signal is

Join networks automatically
If this setting is selected your iPad will connect automatically to wireless networks. This is useful if you move from place to place and have previously joined their network – you will not be prompted each time to re-enter your details. But if you don't want the iPad to join networks automatically, switch this off.

The iPad may join networks that you don't particularly want to join. Tell it to forget certain networks.

Sometimes you don't want the iPad to remember all used networks (hotels, airports, etc.)

1 Go to **Settings > Wi-Fi** and the select the network you want the iPad to forget

2 Click the right arrow

3 Tap **Forget this Network** and it will be deleted from the list

The Preinstalled Apps

App Store

This is the workhorse app on the iPad and gives you access to the online store where you can find thousands more apps to download, covering 24 different categories.

Calendar

This app keeps you organized. It is similar to Calendar on the Mac and Outlook on the PC. The interface is beautiful and it's very easy to enter your appointment details. Usefully, the app's icon shows the current date before you click it to open the app. The Calendar app will be explored more fully in Chapter Nine.

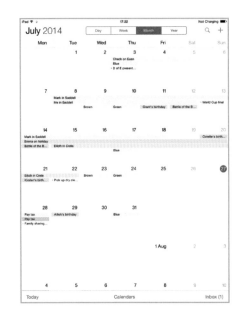

Contacts

This app stores the details
of all your contacts.
Contacts resembles a
physical address book with
left- and right-facing pages.

The app works in both
portrait and landscape
modes.

You can view contacts, add, edit and delete. If you want to add a
photo to a contact this is very easy.

There is smooth integration with Address Book on the Mac and
Outlook on the PC.

Notification Center

As well as messages popping up on your screen from Facebook,
SMS, etc. you can also see all your notifications including
anniversaries and other appointments using the Notification
screen. From any screen simply swipe your finger down the screen
and all your notifications will appear.

Don't forget

Although the
Notification Center itself
is not a preinstalled
app as such, it takes
information from
other apps such as the
Calendar and Reminders.

Mail

Mail is the powerhouse for managing all your email. The Mail app can handle multiple accounts, POP3, IMAP and Exchange (see page 91). The emails are easy to read and HTML is handled well. The app's views vary depending on whether you hold the iPad in portrait or landscape modes.

Mail closely resembles Mail on the Mac.

Hot tip

Some people say they prefer non-HTML email, but HTML email looks much nicer than plain email.

Messages

This is the iPad app for sending text and photo messages (iMessages). In iOS 8 it is also possible to include video and audio clips and also send someone your location on a map.

Notes

This is very similar to Notes on the iPhone and Mac OS X. You can scroll through a list of notes, add new notes, edit, and share using email. You can also sync your notes from the iPad with the Mac and PC using the online iCloud service, if you have an account.

If you find Notes too limiting you can always view the huge variety of third-party apps on the App Store, or you could try a web-based notes service such as Remember The Milk (**rememberthemilk.com**) or Google Tasks.

Newsstand

If you subscribe to newspapers or magazines, this app is where they will end up. Tap the app and browse through your subscriptions.

...cont'd

Videos

The iPad is a gorgeous multimedia device. Its large, high-resolution screen makes videos a joy to watch using the Videos app.

You can watch music videos, movies rented or bought from iTunes or you can copy your own movies across. Plug in a decent pair of headphones and immerse yourself!

Getting your own movies onto the iPad is very easy. See page 120.

iBooks

This is now a presinstalled app on the iPad and it can be used to store your electronic books and also browse the online Store for new titles to download and read.

Reminders

The Reminders app on iOS devices is a welcome addition. The interface is simple and easy to use. Reminders is also available as part of OS X Yosemite and can sync both Mac and iOS devices such as iPad.

Game Center

For all gaming fans, this app can be used to download and play games from the App Store and also play against other people in multi-player games and compare your scores and achievements with other players.

Maps

The Maps app can be used for a variety of uses including looking up locations and destinations, finding directions, locating the addresses of contacts and viewing areas in 3D relief.

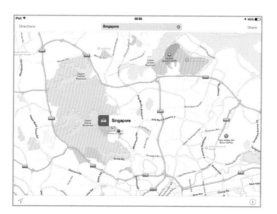

57

The **Settings** app allows you to customize the iPad to suit your specific needs.

...cont'd

Settings app

The Settings app is the central hub for controlling all aspects of your iPad. It is the equivalent to System Preferences on your Mac or Control Panels on the PC. We will explore this in greater detail in Chapter Three.

Use **Settings** for:

- Activating Airplane mode

- Connecting to Wi-Fi

- Setting notifications for individual apps

- Reviewing cellular data usage

- Adjusting the brightness of the screen, and choosing wallpaper

- Setting up Mail, Calendars and Contacts

- Controlling audio, Music, Safari

- Configuring FaceTime

Safari

Although you can download third party browsers from the App Store, Safari is the preinstalled browser on the iPad. It is fast, clean and easy to use. It is very similar to its big brother on the Mac and PC.

You can open several browser windows at the same time and toggle between them.

Bookmarks

You can keep these in sync with Safari on your computer using either iCloud or iTunes.

Safari has an Address Bar/Search box for Google which you can switch to Yahoo! or Bing if you prefer.

Hot tip

If you don't want Google as your search engine – change it to Yahoo! or Bing. Go to **Settings > Safari** and specify your preferred search engine.

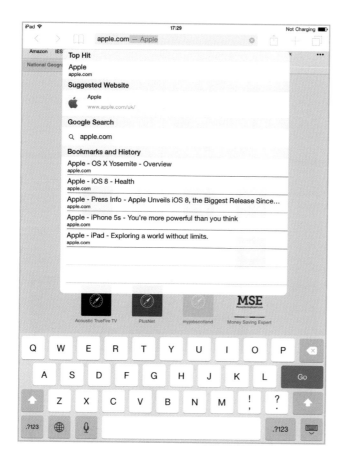

...cont'd

Photos

Visually stunning, the Photos app is perfect for showing off your photos. You can review by Photos or Albums and play slideshows. There is also an option to share specific photos.

iTunes Store

A selection of content, such as music, movies, TV shows and books can be downloaded using the iTunes Store app.

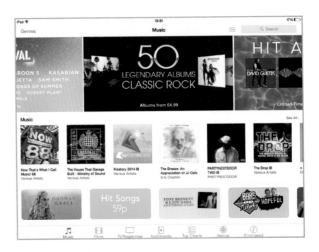

Music

The Music app on the iPad is very similar to the conventional iPod but because the screen real estate is so large, you can view albums and their covers at a larger size, in all their glory! The layout of the screens is very clear, and you can select your music from playlists, albums, artists and several other ways.

Using playlists in the Music app you can gain complete control over your music library.

Podcasts

This is another app that previously had to be downloaded from the App Store but is now presinstalled. It enables you to search for a download audio and video podcasts on a range of topics.

...cont'd

FaceTime

Video chatting is a very personal and interactive way to keep in touch with family and friends around the world. The FaceTime app provides this facility with other iPad, iPhone and iPod Touch users, or a Mac computer with FaceTime. To use FaceTime for video chatting:

What do you need?

 iPad with FaceTime and a Wi-Fi or cellular connection

 The other person needs FaceTime on their iPhone, iPad, or Mac. They also need to be on Wi-Fi or cellular network

 Apple ID (i.e. iTunes account, iCloud)

Using FaceTime

 Launch **FaceTime**

 Sign in if not already signed in (you don't need to do this each time)

 Tap **Contacts** and find the person you want to FaceTime chat with

 Tap their **email address** or cell phone number (the latter will start a FaceTime call using their iPhone

 Add to favorites if you plan to call this person regularly

 Tap a contact in the **Video** tab to return a recent FaceTime call

Photo Booth

As the name suggests, this app lets you take photos of yourself as if you were in a photo booth. It also has several built-in effects which distort the image.

 Launch **Photo Booth**

 Choose the effect you want to use, e.g. Thermal Camera, X-ray etc. If you want a standard image choose Normal

3 Tap the **shutter button** at the bottom and the Photo Booth will take a picture which will be added to your camera roll

Tips

This is a new app for iOS 8 and it offers a range of help advice about using it and the apps that are on the iPad. The tips are updated on a regular basis so it is always worth looking at it from time to time.

Back up your iPad regularly so you have a recent backup with which to perform a restore if things go badly wrong or if your iPad is lost or stolen!

Hot tip

If you have iCloud activated, all of the items that you have selected here will also by synced automatically to the iCloud, when you are connected to the Internet via Wi-Fi.

Hot tip

Reset the iPad if it misbehaves.

Restore and Reset the iPad

Your entire iPad contents will be backed up every time you sync with your computer – iTunes takes care of this. For that reason, you should perform regular syncs with your computer, even if you don't want to update the content.

If the iPad misbehaves and you need to restore it you will need a recent backup file to use for the restore.

Restoring the iPad erases the iPad and copies all of your apps, settings, and data from the restore file which iTunes will have created for you (*providing you have synced recently!*).

To restore iPad

 Connect the iPad to the computer

 Make sure iTunes is open and select your iPad when it appears in iTunes under **Devices**

 Select the **Summary** tab

 Select the **Restore** option

 When prompted to back up your settings before restoring, select the **Back Up** option. If you have performed a recent backup you can ignore this

Resetting the iPad
If you have an iPhone you may be familiar with the reset option.

 Hold down the **Home button + On/Off** button for several seconds

 The screen will go black and the Apple logo will appear on the screen

 Let go of the buttons now

The iPad should boot up. Any problems you had before should have been corrected. If not, try **restoring** the iPad.

3 iPad Settings

The whole look and feel of the iPad is controlled through Settings, one of the apps preinstalled on the iPad. In this chapter we will look at all settings, from wallpapers to the Music app, getting things set up perfectly for optimal use.

Up in the Air

The iPad is a great multimedia device for listening to music or watching movies on the plane. There are strict rules about wireless and cellular receivers – these must be switched off during the flight. Airplane Mode switches all iPad radios off. Airplane mode is only seen with the Wi-Fi and cellular models.

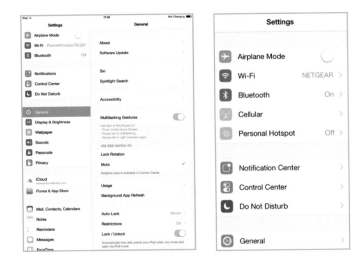

Settings on Wi-Fi model   Settings on Wi-Fi + cellular model

Wi-Fi only models

 Go to **Settings > Wi-Fi**. Turn Wi-Fi **Off** by tapping the **On/Off** button or sliding the slider to the right

 Wi-Fi is now fully off. You cannot receive Wi-Fi signals and the iPad is safe to use on the plane

Wi-Fi and cellular models

 Go to **Settings > Airplane Mode** and push the slider to the right

 Wi-Fi and cellular radios are now fully off

For both models, when you are off the plane, go back to settings and slide the slider to the left which switches the radios back on.

Getting Online with Wi-Fi

The iPad is designed to be used online – using either a wireless connection or cellular network. You can use it without Internet access but you won't be able to browse online content, download apps, content, or update your apps.

Connect to a wireless network

1 Open **Settings > Wi-Fi**

2 Make sure Wi-Fi is set to **On**

3 Choose a network: you will see a list of available networks near you. If locked (most are) you will see a padlock symbol. Some networks may appear "open" and let you connect but when you browse you will be presented with a request for username and password

4 Tap the name of the network you want to connect to

5 Enter the password if you know it

6 You should see a check mark next to the network name showing which wireless network you have joined

7 If your network is hidden but you know its name tap **Other...**

8 You can allow the iPad to join networks quietly without alerting you (**Ask to Join Networks Off**) or you may prefer to be asked before the iPad joins a network (**Ask to Join Networks On**)

Hot tip

No Wi-Fi connection? If you have an iPhone, switch on **Personal Hotspot** (**Settings > Personal Hotspot**). This lets the iPad use the iPhone's cellular connection. Be careful – the data used comes out of your iPhone allowance!

67

...cont'd

9 You can see the strength of the connection by checking the wireless icon at the top left of the iPad display or in the wireless connection window (in **Settings**)

Setting network connection manually

1 Tap the blue i symbol to the right of the network name

2 You can choose an IP Address using **DHCP**, **BootIP**, or **Static Address. Subnet Mask, Router, DNS**, and **Search Domains** are also shown in the window though you won't need to change these

3 If you use a proxy to get onto the Internet, enter the details manually or set to **Auto**. Most people don't use proxies so it is unlikely you'll need to change anything here

Don't forget

Another network setting is for switching Bluetooth on or off for sharing content over short distances with radio connectivity.

Setting Up Notifications

If you have used the iPhone you will be familiar with notifications. These are audio and visual alerts used by some apps. For example, if you use a messaging app you may want to see how many unread messages there are without actually opening the app. Or, if you use an app like Skype, you may want to be shown on screen when someone is calling you even when the iPad screen is locked. By setting up your notifications you can choose how much or how little information you receive in terms of messages, calls, updates, etc.

Set up notifications

1 Open **Settings > Notifications**

2 Under the **Include** heading you will see a list of apps that use Notifications

3 To configure Notifications for an app, tap its name in the list. You can then turn On or Off the **Allow Notifications** option and set a sound and style for how these notifications appear in the Notification Center

Hot tip

Spend some time setting up your **Notifications** to avoid unwanted intrusions by apps sending useless notifications!

Some apps offer notification by **Sounds, Alerts** and **Badges**. Sounds **On** means the iPad will play a sound when a notification is received. Alerts are messages that display on the screen, and Badges are the red circles that appear at the top right of the app's icon when notifications have been received.

If you want to keep intrusion from notifications to a minimum, switch adjust the settings on an app-by-app basis.

Cellular Data

This is only shown in the Wi-Fi and cellular model.

Check cellular data

1 Go to **Settings > Cellular**

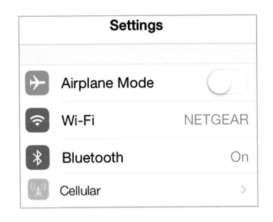

2 Make sure Cellular Data is **On**

You may want to use **Data Roaming** to get online if you are away from your home country. *Note*: roaming charges for Internet access are high so be careful if you switch this to ON. In general, it is better to leave this switched OFF!

- You can view your account, review your data plan, **Add Data** or **Change Plan** (from pay-as-you-go to monthly), and Edit User Information

- **APN Settings** will vary depending on your carrier

- You can set up a **SIM PIN**

- Under **SIM Applications** you will see lots of services provided by your cellular carrier

Beware

When abroad, keep Data Roaming OFF or your phone bill may be huge – the cost of data download outside your own country is generally very high. Or you may be very wealthy in which case you can switch it on!

Set Up Your Wallpaper

Just like your Mac or PC, you can change the picture displayed at the Lock Screen and the background you see behind the apps. You can alter both of these using the in-built iPad wallpapers or you can use your own pictures.

Apple has already provided some excellent images but you may want more. There are several websites offering wallpapers and one of the best is **interfacelift.com** which offers stunning photos for Mac and PC – these should work on the iPad as well.

Changing the wallpaper

 Go to **Settings > Wallpaper**

 Tap on the **Choose a New Wallpaper** option

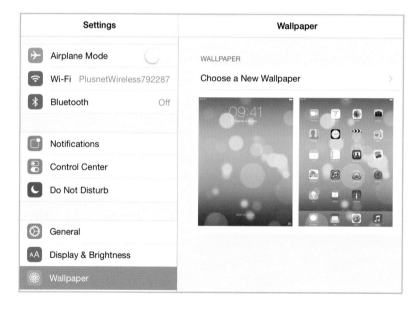

There are 39 different Apple backgrounds that can be used for wallpaper. These include **Dynamic** backgrounds that appear to move independently from the apps icon layer above, and **Stills** backgrounds.

71

The **Display & Brightness** setting can be used to change the screen brightness and also change the font size, for apps that support this feature.

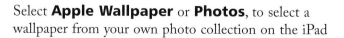 Select **Apple Wallpaper** or **Photos**, to select a wallpaper from your own photo collection on the iPad

Tap to make your choice and decide whether you want the new image as only wallpaper or Lock Screen or both

General Settings

About

This provides full information about your iPad, serial number, number of apps installed, songs, and much more.

Software Update

This can be used to check the version of iOS that you are using and install updates if they are available.

Siri

Use this to set the language and voice style for the Siri voice assistant function.

Spotlight Search

Determines the types of items that appear in the Spotlight Search window.

Accessibility

Use this to set a variety of accessibility features for vision, hearing, learning and physical and motor conditions.

Multitasking Gestures

This setting allows you to pinch to activate the Home screen, swipe up (four fingers) to reveal the Multitasking bar (or also click twice on the Home button) or swipe left or right between running apps.

Use Side Switch to:

You can configure the Side Switch to lock rotation, or activate the Mute function. (The Side Switch is not included on the iPad Air 2 but it is on all other models of iPad).

Usage

This tells you how much data you have sent and received. You can also switch Battery Percentage on here.

Background App Refresh

This can be used to allow apps to be updated automatically when your iPad has online access through Wi-Fi or a cellular service.

Don't forget

There is a specific setting for **Sounds**, where you can configure the alert sounds for new mail arriving, sent mail, calendar and social networking app alerts, lock sounds and keyboard clicks.

72

Auto-Lock

This locks the screen if there is no input after a set period. You can select between 2-15 minutes or Never. Something around five minutes is probably the most practical. Once the autolock is activated you will need to re-enter your four-digit PIN at the Lock Screen to use the iPad.

Restrictions

Useful if the iPad will be used by children. You can limit access to specific apps and also prohibit the installation of apps.

Lock/Unlock

This can be used to automatically lock or unlock your iPad, through the use of an iPad cover.

Date & Time

Choose the 12- or 24-hour clock. Set Time Zone, Date and Time.

Keyboard

Here you can enable and disable Auto-Correction, Auto-Capitalization of the first letter in sentences, Enable Caps Lock and "." Shortcut (two taps on spacebar generates a period).

Language & Region

This allows you to select keyboards in different languages.

iTunes Wi-Fi Sync

This can be used to automatically sync the contents of your iPad with iTunes on your computer, when your iPad is connected to Wi-Fi. In iTunes on your computer you have to also check on **Sync with this iPad over Wi-Fi**.

VPN

Lets you see your VPN (Virtual Private Network) connection if you use one, or the wireless network to which you are connected.

Reset

Use this to reset a setting all of your iPad settings, network settings, the keyboard, the Home screen layout and location and privacy settings.

Passcode

This is now an individual setting. It prevents people accessing your iPad and its data by creating a password for the lock screen.

On the latest models of iPad that have a Touch ID sensor, the iPad Air 2 and the iPad Mini 3, the setting **Touch ID & Passcode** can be used to set up the Touch ID for the Home button so that your iPad can only be unlocked by your own unique fingerprint.

Mail, Contacts, Calendars

This is the hub that lets you set up your email accounts, your contacts and your calendars.

Mail

1 Tap **Settings > Mail, Contacts, Calendars**

2 Tap **Add Account...**

3 Decide which type to use if you know this. You can choose from Microsoft Exchange, iCloud, Google Mail, Yahoo! Mail, or AOL. If you are uncertain, tap Other...

4 Enter your full name, email address and password

5 Give the account a **Description**, e.g. "Work Email"

6 Click **Save** and Mail will configure the account for you

Accounts

You can configure Mail to switch on Mail, Contacts, Calendars and Bookmarks for iCloud (cloud) syncing. You can also switch **Find My iPad** to On if you want to use this feature.

You will see the account information displayed under **Settings > Mail, Contacts, Calendars > Accounts.**

Review the settings for the Mail app

Preview – how many lines of the email do you want to preview?

Show To/Cc Label – show or hide this option

Swipe Option – tap on this for options for what appears when you swipe left or right on an email in your Inbox

Flag Style – this determines the color and shape of flags that are used on emails

Ask Before Deleting – switch to **On** as a safety measure, preventing the unwanted deletion of emails

Hot tip

Find My iPad is free so set it up and use it if you lose your iPad.

Load Remote Images – if an email contains images and you want to see these, switch to **On**

Organize By Thread – drag this **On** to view email conversations combined into individual threads

Always Bcc Myself – for blind copies sent to yourself

Mark Addresses – use this to add flags to certain types of email addresses

Increase Quote Level – this indents messages that you forward to people

Signature – assign a signature for the end of each email

Contacts

There are few settings to configure here:

Sort Order – sort your contacts by first or last name

Display Order – same as above

Show in App Switcher – turn this **On** to show your recent contacts at the top of the App Switcher (Multitasking) window

Short Name – select the format for abbreviated names

My Info – view your own details within the **Contacts** app

Calendars

Time Zone Override – switch to **Off** to display events for your current location

Alternate Calendars – select calendars for different languages

Week Numbers – Turn **On** to show week numbers for the current year, at the start of the week

Show Invitee Declines – show any declined calendar invites

Sync – set a timescale for syncing your calendar events

Default Alert Times – set alerts times for certain events

Start Week On – set a day for your calendar to start on

Default Calendar – select the default calendar for new events

Safari Settings

You can customize a lot of settings on the Safari web browser. Tap **Settings > Safari** and select from the following:

Search Engine – select Google, Yahoo!, Bing or DuckDuckGo

Search Engine Suggestions – use this to display suggestions as you type into the Address bar or a search engine

Spotlight Suggestions – use this to display suggestions as you type into the Spotlight search box

Quick Website Search – turn this **On** to use the Smart Search Field for searching using a website name and then a specific keyword, to search for it on the selected website

Preload Top Hit – use this to enable Safari to start loading the top result from a search, to make it quicker to access it

Passwords & AutoFill – use this to remember your passwords and details entered into forms

Favorites – use this for what is displayed on the Favorites page, when you open a new tab or enter an address in the Address bar

Open New Tabs in Background – use this if you want to open new tabs while you are still viewing the current page

Show Favorites Bar – use this to show or hide the Favorites bar (this is displayed at the top of the Safari window)

Show Tab Bar – use this to show all open tabs on the Tab Bar

Block Pop-ups – leave **On** to avoid annoying pop-ups

Do Not Track – turn this **On** if you do not want any details of your web browsing to be stored

Block Cookies – many sites insist on allowing cookies but you can clear all the cookies (see Clear History and Website Data)

Fraudulent Website Warning – it is wise to be alerted when you visit potentially fraudulent sites so leave this **On**

Clear History and Website Data – tap on this to delete details of your web browsing history and stored website data

Advanced – a range of advanced settings, such as for clearing website data and using JavaScript

Hot tip

AutoFill is useful and saves you having to type your personal details on websites.

More Settings

Maps

Distances – whether distances on maps are shown in kilometers or miles

Map Labels – turn labels in English on or off

Music

Sound Check – this evens out the volume so that tracks will play back at the same volume

EQ – sets the equalizer which enhances the audio output

Volume Limit – prevents hearing damage by limiting the volume of playback, keeping it at a safe level

Group By Album Artist – keep albums by the same artists together

Show All Music – display all of the available music in the app

Genius – use this to anonymously share information about your music library with Apple and enable suggestions, based on your previous choices and preferences

iTunes Match – any music on your iPad that is on iTunes is added to iCloud so you can listen to it on any device

Videos

Start Playing – the default is sensibly set to **Where I Left Off** so you can stop watching a movie and resume later

Show All Videos – display all of the available videos within the app

The **Notes** and **Reminders** apps also have their own Settings.

There is a range of **Privacy** settings where you can turn on **Location Services** so that specific apps can use your current geographic location.

...cont'd

FaceTime

Enter the email address you want to use with FaceTime. If you don't want to be contacted using FaceTime you can switch it off

Photos & Camera

Sharing options – select options for sharing your photos to your own devices with iCloud and your Photo Stream (for more details, see Chapter Six, page 117)

Photos Tab – turn this on or off to show or hide summaries of your photos

Slideshow – use these options to determine how long each slide is played for, to repeat a slideshow and shuffle the photos in a slideshow

Camera – use to turn a grid on or off for the camera, to help with composing photos

High Dynamic Range – use this to blend the best exposures from three photos, while keeping the originals too

iTunes & App Store

This is where you set up your account details for the iTunes Store.

Tap on the account name to see your details, including address, phone number, and credit card.

Automatic Downloads – select which items out of Music, Apps, Books and Updates you want to be downloaded automatically, when you are connected to online services over Wi-Fi

Don't forget

There are also settings for social networking sites, including Facebook and Twitter, that enable you to log in to these accounts and link them to iOS 8.

Hot tip

Setting up iTunes alerts is not obvious. To set up alerts go to **Settings > iTunes & App Store** then tap **Apple ID**. Then tap **View Apple ID**. Sign in with your password and scroll down to **My Alerts**. Set up your alerts from the options shown.

4 Browsing the Web

Browsing the Web is probably the most popular activity on desktop and laptop computers so it comes as no surprise that the same is true of the iPad. Safari is preinstalled on the iPad and is a clean, fast browser that will more than satisfy all of your browsing needs.

Around Safari

The Safari app is the default web browser on the iPad. This can be used to view web pages, save favorites and read pages with the Reader function. To start using Safari:

 Tap on the **Safari** app

 Tap on the Address Bar at the top of the Safari window. Type a web page address

Hot tip

When you type in the Safari Address Bar the Favorites window appears from where you can select one of your favorite or bookmarked web pages.

 Tap on the **Go** button on the keyboard to open the web page, or select one of the options below the Address Bar

Go

Don't forget

When a page opens in Safari a blue status bar underneath the page name indicates the progress of the loading page.

⊗   Apple

The selected page opens with the top toolbar visible. As you scroll down the page this disappears to give you a greater viewing area. Tap on the top of the screen or scroll back up to display the toolbar again

Navigating Pages

When you are viewing pages within Safari there are a number of functions that can be used:

 1 Tap on these buttons to move forward and back between web pages that have been visited

 2 Tap here to view Bookmarked pages, Reading List pages and Shared Links

3 Tap here to add a bookmark, add to a reading list, add an icon to your iPad Home screen, email a link to a page, Tweet a page, send it to Facebook or print a page

4 Tap here to add a new tab

5 Tap on a link on a page to open it. Tap and hold to access additional options, to open in a new tab, add to a Reading List or copy the link

6 Tap and hold on an image and tap on **Save Image** or **Copy**

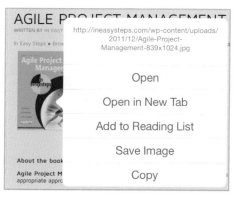

Hot tip

Tap and hold on the **Forward** and **Back** buttons to view lists of previously-visited pages in these directions.

Hot tip

The **Reading List** is similar to bookmarks and you can use it to save pages that you want to read later. Also, you can read them when you are offline. The Reading List can be accessed from the button in Step 2.

Opening New Tabs

Safari supports tabbed browsing, which means that you can open separate pages within the same window and access them by tapping on each tab at the top of the page:

 Tap here to open a new tab for another page

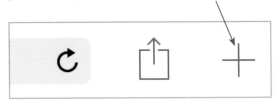

The items that appear in the Favorites window can be determined within **Settings > Safari** and tapping on the **Favorites** link.

2 Open a new page by entering a web address into the Address Bar, or tap on one of the thumbnails in the **Favorites** window

If there are too many items to be displayed on the Favorites Bar, tap on this button to view the other items.

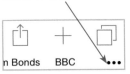

3 Tap on the tab headings to move between tabbed pages

4 Tap on the cross at the top of a tab to close it

Tab View

A previous feature of the iOS operating system on the iPhone was the ability to view all of your open Safari tabs on one screen. In iOS 8 this functionality has also come to the iPad with Tab View. To use this:

 1 Tap here to activate Tab View

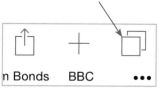

2 All of the currently open tabs are displayed. Tap on one to open it

Tab View can also be activated by pinching inwards with thumb and forefinger on a web page that is at normal magnification, i.e. 1 to 1.

3 If you have open Safari tabs on other Apple devices, these will shown at the bottom of the window

Don't forget

Tap on the **Done** button at the top of the Tab View window to exit this and return to the web page that was being viewed when Tab View was activated.

4 Tap on this button at the top of the window to open another tab

5 Tap on this button to open a **Private** tab, where no browsing record will be recorded during this browsing session

Private

Bookmarking Pages

Once you start using Safari you will soon build up a collection of favorite pages that you visit regularly. To access these quickly they can be bookmarked so that you can then go to them in one tap. To set up and use bookmarks:

1 Open a web page that you want to bookmark. Tap here to access the sharing options

2 Tap on the **Add Bookmark** button

3 Tap on this link and select whether to include the bookmark on the Favorites Bar or in a Bookmarks folder

4 Tap on the **Save** button

5 Tap here to view all of the bookmarks. The Bookmarks folders are listed. Tap on the **Edit** button at the bottom of the panel to delete or rename the folders

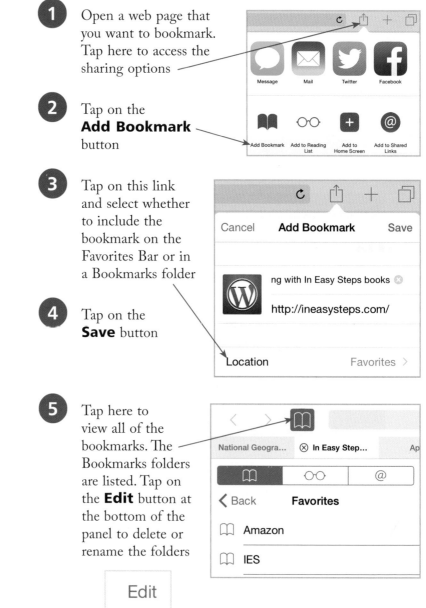

Don't forget

The Favorites Bar appears underneath the Address Bar in Safari. This includes items that have been added as bookmarks.

Safari History

All of your browsing will leave a history trail behind. This is useful if you want to revisit sites (*you should have saved a bookmark!*). Over time, the history list will become huge so it's a good idea to clear this from time to time. In addition, other people using your iPad can see your history and there may be sites you visit which you would prefer to keep private!

Clear the history

1 Go to **Settings > Safari**

2 Tap **Clear History and Website Data**

3 You will be asked to confirm this action

4 Tap **Clear** and the history will be cleared

Add Links to Home Screen

The various iPad screens are home to all of your apps, but you can also add web pages as buttons to the Home screen to make finding and opening these easier. You wouldn't want all of your saved websites to be added to the Home screen or you would have no room for actual apps. But for websites that are very important, or that you visit regularly, consider adding them to the Home screen.

 Navigate to a site you want to save

 Tap the **Share** icon

 Choose **Add to Home Screen**

 Name the saved link and tap on the **Add** button

The web page will resemble an app on the Home screen

Tap it and it will open Safari and take you straight to the correct web page

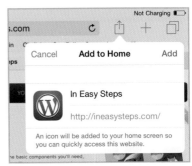

Safari Privacy

We have already looked at the History and clearing this from time to time. The other item worth clearing on the iPad (and regular computer browsers, for that matter) is the Cookies file. This is a file containing sites you have visited and the entries are made by the sites themselves. They don't necessarily do any major harm but for reasons of privacy it is a good idea to clear Cookies periodically.

 Go to **Settings > Safari** – Tap **Block Cookies**

For peace of mind, clear Cookies and Cache from time to time, as described on page 85.

2 Select one of the options for blocking cookies

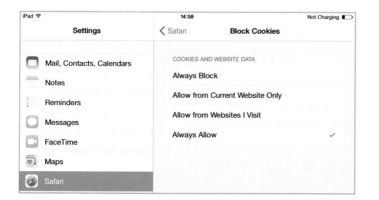

Other Web Browsers

Safari is the default pre-installed browser on the iPad but there are others which include:

- Opera Mini (*shown below*)
- Atomic Web
- Privately
- Mercury Web Browser
- Safe Browser
- Browser plus

Some of these are written specifically for the iPad while others are for the iPhone but can be used on the iPad.

What are the advantages of using third-party browsers?

- Many offer private browsing (no history retained)
- If you get bored with Safari and fancy a change try out one of these other ones and see if it suits your needs better

5 Mail and Text

Love it or loathe it, email is a fact of life. We need to deal with email at work and at home. Mail on the iPad makes reading and sending emails a pleasure and in this chapter we will look at how to set up your accounts, manage your Inbox, and make the most of IMAP email.

What is Mail?

We spend much of our time on PCs and Macs checking and sending emails. This is true also of mobile devices like the iPhone, BlackBerry and other handhelds. So, not surprisingly, a fair amount of your time on the iPad may be spent doing emails.

The Mail app built in to the iPad is a feature-rich program that is easy to set up and use. It is similar to Mail, which comes with every Mac PowerBook and Mac desktop, although a few features are lacking. There's no stationery option on the iPad version and you can't have multiple signatures.

Setting up an Email Account

1 Go to **Settings > Mail, Contacts, Calendars** and tap on the **Add Account** link

2 You will see a list of options

3 Choose the one that matches your email account

4 If you can't see it, select **Other** – enter your details including email address and password. The program will work out the rest for you

POP or IMAP?

For most people these are fairly confusing terms but it's worth having a look at both types before setting your accounts up. POP stands for *Post Office Protocol* and IMAP means *Internet Message Access Protocol*. These are the two most common standards for email retrieval. POP3 is the current version of POP and is used for web-based email such as Google Mail. Rather than look at the nuts and bolts of these two systems we can summarize the pros and cons of each.

IMAP lets you see all of your emails using any machine

If you use multiple computers – including handhelds such as BlackBerry or iPad – IMAP allows you to see your various mail folders from any device. The folder structure and the emails within the folders are the same because the folders and emails are kept on a central server (*not* on your computer or iPad).

iPad 🔋		
	Mailboxes	Edit
🖾 Inbox		4 >
★ VIP		ⓘ >
MAILBOXES		
🗋 Drafts		7 >
◁ Sent		>

When you set up a POP3 account you will see folders for Inbox, Sent Mail, Trash but no subfolders or the opportunity to create subfolders to categorize and file your emails. But with an IMAP account you can create as many folders and subfolders (and sub-subfolders) as you like and file all of your emails. You can browse all of your IMAP folders and emails on the iPad and transfer new emails into their respective folders, just as you would with paper mail using a file cabinet. There is a downside to IMAP though – since the emails are stored on a server which may be in the US (iCloud emails are currently stored in California) if you have no Internet connection you may not be able to see your emails.

So, which should you use?

If your email provider, e.g. Apple (iCloud), provides IMAP then select that. If POP3 is the only option you have, there's not much you can do to change this. For those of us wishing to archive emails and retrieve them months or years later IMAP is the best possible solution.

Hot tip

For Mail, IMAP email offers many advantages over POP3.

Composing an Email

1 Open **Mail** by tapping its icon and decide which account you want to use (if you have more than one) by tapping **Accounts** and choosing the one you want to use

2 Tap the **New email** icon

3 Enter the name of the recipient. As you start typing, Mail will present you with a list of possible options. Choose the recipient from the list if it's there

4 Tap the **Subject** box and enter subject here

5 Tap the main body of the email and type the text of your email

Hot tip

You can add signatures to your emails (Go to **Settings > Mail, Contacts, Calendars > Signature**). You can choose one generic signature or create a specific signature for each email account.

Type (or use Voice Dictation – see icon to left of keyboard if on Wi-Fi)

Mail will spot mistakes and suggest the correct word

6 If you want to copy someone in on the email use the **Cc** box. To send a blind copy (the email recipient cannot see that a blind copy has been sent to another person, hence the term "blind") tap the **Bcc** box

7 Check the **spelling** – any errors will be underlined with a red dotted line. Correct by tapping on the misspelled word and choosing from available options, or delete the word and retype if Mail does not offer the correct word

8 Once you're happy with the content and spelling tap **Send** and your email will be sent

Attach files to an email

At present you cannot attach files in the same way as you would with a regular computer – there's no real "desktop" or filing system you can see in order to find and attach a file. However, it can be done by pressing and holding within an email, see tip.

You can also send files such as documents and photos by email from *within* an app.

For example, in the Photos app there is an option to share photos by email. You can email Safari web pages from within the Safari app, and document management programs like Documents To Go allow you to email files from within the Documents To Go app.

Hot tip

You can add a photo or a video directly into an email by pressing and holding in the body of the email and tapping on the **Insert Photo or Video** button. You can then select the required item from the Photos app.

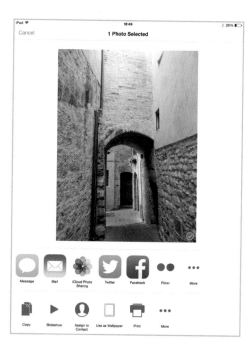

Here, a photo has been opened in Photos. To email the photo, tap the Share icon (bottom left) and select **Mail** from the dropdown menu options.

This option can be found in many apps on the iPad.

Receiving and Reading Emails

Emails are "pushed" to the iPad from the email server if your iPad is online. You can tell there are unread emails by looking for the badge on the app's icon.

Manually checking for email
You can make Mail check for new email by pulling down on the email list.

Reading emails in portrait mode
If you hold the iPad in portrait mode you will see a separate floating account window listing emails in the Inbox.

 Tap an email in the list and it will fill the whole screen

 To see the next or previous email tap the down or up arrows ∧ ∨ or tap Inbox again. Next to the word **Inbox** you may see (3) which means you have three unread emails in the Inbox

 When reading emails you can: **Move** the email ▭ **Delete** 🗑, **Reply or Reply All** ↩, **Forward** the email to someone else ↩, **Compose** a new email ✐ and Flag an email ⚑

Reading emails in landscape mode

 Tap the email you want to read – it will be displayed in the right pane

 If you want to navigate to other folders in your account, tap the name of the account (top left) and you will see a folder list

 Scroll up or down until you find the folder you want then tap it. You will then see the emails contained within that folder

Hot tip

Manual send and receive will save power. It is also the best way to retrieve email if you are using Data Roaming.

94

4 Navigate back up the hierarchy by tapping the account name at the top

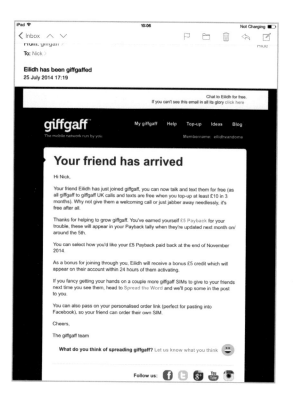

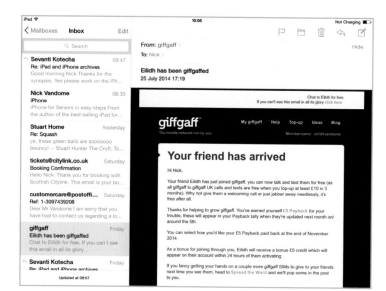

Searching for Emails

Mail provides a simple search box at the top left below the account name. You can search: **From, To, Subject, All.**

Searching for emails is usually quicker than looking for them manually.

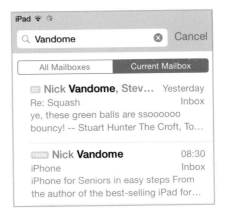

Searching for emails across multiple accounts
You can also search for emails using the Spotlight search:

 Go to **Spotlight** search (press and hold on an empty space on a Home screen and swipe downwards)

 Enter your search terms into the search box

 Spotlight will then search all of your emails (and will search Calendars, Contacts, Music, etc. unless you have configured Spotlight so it only searches emails)

 Once the email you are looking for is listed in the search list, tap it and Mail will open and will take you to that email which will open on the screen

Deleting Unwanted Emails

We all receive email spam or emails we don't want to keep.
It's easy to delete emails, either singly or in batches.

Delete a single email

1 If the email you want to delete is open on the
screen, simply tap the **Trash** icon and the email
will be sucked into the trash folder

2 If you are looking at a list of emails in the account
window, tap **Edit** then tap the radio button next to the
email you want to delete. Then hit **Trash**. The brackets
with (1) tell you that one email has been selected for
Delete or Move

3 Another way of deleting emails is to view the list in the
accounts window then drag your finger across the email
from right to left and a **Trash** button will appear. Tap
this and the email will be deleted

Hot tip

Tap on the **More** button
in Step 3 to access more
options, including moving
the email to Junk. Tap
on the **Flag** button to
add a flag to the email,
to make it easier to find.

Retrieve Deleted Emails

Have my emails gone forever?

You may accidentally delete an email you wanted to keep. You can get this back!

 Tap the **Name** of the account

 Tap **Trash**. Look down the list for emails you want to recover from the Trash

 Tap **Edit**

 Tap the **radio button** of the email you want to recover

 Tap **Move**

 Choose **Inbox**

 The message will move from Trash → Inbox

Panic over!

Don't forget

Deleted emails can usually be salvaged from the Trash if you want to recover them.

Get Organized!

Filing emails

1 With the email open tap the **Folder** icon

2 Decide which account you want to use to store the email (in this example **Business**)

🗀	Apple
🗀	Business
🗀	Family

3 Tap on the folder name and the email will move across into its new location

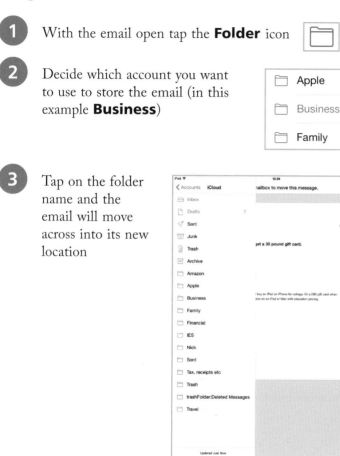

4 Move back to the main account level and tap on the folder name to view its contents

Adding Mailboxes

Different categories of email messages can be managed via Mailboxes. For instance, you may want to keep your social emails separately from ones that apply to financial activities.

 From your Inbox, tap on the **Mailboxes** button

 The current mailboxes are displayed. Tap on **Edit**

Hot tip

Messages can be edited within individual mailboxes. To do this, select a mailbox and tap once on the **Edit** button. The message can then be edited with the **Delete**, **Move** or **Mark** options at the bottom of the window.

 Tap on **New Mailbox** at the bottom of the Mailboxes panel

New Mailbox

 Enter a name for the new mailbox. Tap on the **Save** button

Tap on the **Done** button

Done

To delete a mailbox, tap on it, then tap on the **Delete Mailbox** button

Messaging

Text messaging is now a commonly used method for keeping in touch. On your iPad you can join the world of text with the Apple iMessage service that is accessed via the Messages app. This enables text and media messages to be sent, free of charge, between users of the iOS (from version 5 onwards) operating systems, on the iPad, iPhone and iPod Touch. iMessages can be sent to cell/mobile phone numbers and email addresses. To use iMessages:

 Tap once on the **Messages** app

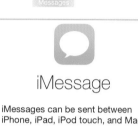

You have to sign in with your Apple ID before you can use Messages. Enter these details and tap on the **Sign In** button

Beware

If a number, or an email address, is not recognized it shows up in red in the **To** box.

Tap once on this button to create a new message and start a new conversation

Tap once on this button to select someone from your contacts

Tap once on a contact to select them as the recipient of the new message

...cont'd

Creating iMessages

To create and edit messages and conversations:

1 Tap once here and type with the keyboard to create a message. Tap once on the **Send** button

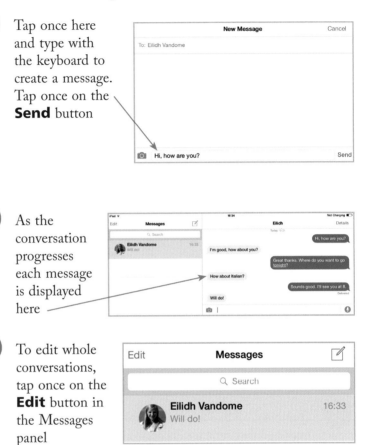

Hot tip

Press and hold on a message and tap on the **More** button that appears. Select a message, or messages, and tap on the **Trash** icon to remove them.

2 As the conversation progresses each message is displayed here

3 To edit whole conversations, tap once on the **Edit** button in the Messages panel

Edit

Don't forget

When a message has been sent you are notified underneath it if has been delivered.

4 Tap once here and tap once on the **Delete** button to delete the conversation

Delete

Sending Photos and Videos

Within Messages in iOS 8 it is possible to add different types of media to a text message, including photos and videos. To do this:

1. To add a photo or a video, tap once on the camera icon next to the text field. Select an item from your **Photo Library** or take a photo or video

2. The Camera apps opens. Select the photo or video option and capture by tapping on the shutter button

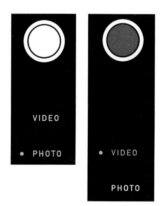

If you do not like a photo or video that you have taken, tap once on the **Retake** button and try again.

3. Tap once on the **Use Photo** or **Use Video** button

4. The photo or video is added to the text field, where new text can also be added

...cont'd

Adding Audio Clips

You can also send family and friends audio messages in an iMessage so that they can hear from you too. To do this:

 Press and hold on the microphone icon at the right-hand side of the text field

 Create your audio clip and tap once here to send it

3 Tap once here to delete the current clip and start recording again

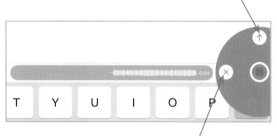

Sending your location

With Messages you can now also show people your location (by sending a map) rather than just telling them. To do this:

1 Once a conversation has started, tap once on the **Details** button

2 Tap once on the **Send My Current Location**, or **Share My Location** buttons

LOCATION

Send My Current Location

Share My Location

3 For Share My Location, tap once on one of the options for how long you want your location to be shared for

Share for One Hour

Share Until End of Day

Share Indefinitely

Hot tip

If you select **Share My Location**, this will be updated if your location changes (as long as Location Services are turned On, **Settings > Privacy > Location Services**).

6 Photos

The iPad app, Photos, *delivers rich-looking photos at high resolution so you can view all of your albums as slideshows or share them with family and friends.*

Getting Photos onto the iPad

Because of its high resolution display and rich colors, the iPad is perfect for viewing photos. The iPad supports pictures in a number of formats including JPEG, TIFF, GIF and PNG. But how do you get your photos onto the iPad in the first place, in addition to using either of the two iPad cameras?

Importing from a computer program

 You can import from iPhoto or Aperture on the Mac or from Adobe Photoshop Album 2.0 or later, or Adobe Photoshop Elements 3.0 or later

 Use iTunes to configure which albums you want to sync and also remove from selected albums

Using the Lightning to SD Card Camera Reader

 Plug in the Lightning to SD Card Camera Reader

 Insert the SD card from your camera

 Click **Import Photos**

 You will be asked whether you want to keep or delete the photos on the SD card

 View your photos by tapping the **Photos** app

Using the Lightning to USB Camera Adapter

 Plug the Lightning to USB Camera Adapter into the iPad

 Attach the camera using the camera cable

 Make sure the camera is turned **On** and is in transfer mode

 Select the photos you want to import

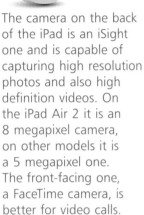

The camera on the back of the iPad is an iSight one and is capable of capturing high resolution photos and also high definition videos. On the iPad Air 2 it is an 8 megapixel camera, on other models it is a 5 megapixel one. The front-facing one, a FaceTime camera, is better for video calls.

When importing photos from a camera you can also choose whether to keep the photos on the camera once they have been imported, or delete them.

Adding Photos from Email

You can email a photo to yourself or add any photos you have received in an email.

 Open the email containing the photo or image

 Make sure you can see the image you want to import then tap and hold your finger on the image until you see a pop-up saying **Message, Mail, Twitter, Facebook, Flickr, iCloud Sharing, Quick Look, Save Image, Assign to Contact, Print, Copy**

3 Tap **Save Image** and the image will be sent to the **Photos** app on the iPad

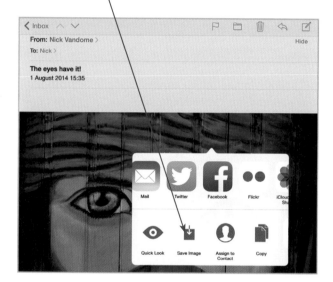

Saving photos or images from Safari web pages

1 Tap and hold your finger on the image you want to save

2 Hold your finger on the image until you see a pop-up saying **Save Image/Copy**

3 The image will be sent to the **Photos** app on the iPad

Viewing Photos

Once photos have been captured they can be viewed and organized in the Photos app. To do this:

1 Tap on the **Photos** app

2 At the top level, all photos are displayed according to the years in which they were taken

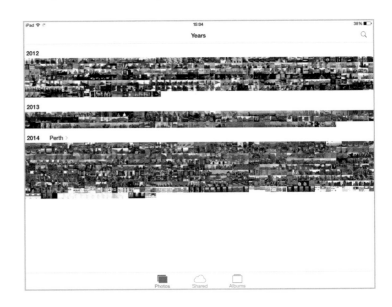

Hot tip

If you have iCloud set up, all of your photos will also be saved under the **All Photos** album in the **Albums** section. This enables all of your photos to be made available on any other devices you have with iCloud, such as an iPhone, an iPod Touch or a Mac computer.

Don't forget

Tap on the **Photos**, **Shared** and **Albums** buttons at the bottom of the **Years**, **Collections** or **Moments** windows, to view the photos in each of these sections.

3 Tap within the **Years** window to view photos according to specific, more defined, timescales. This is the **Collections** level

4 Tap within the Collections window to drill down further into the photos, within the **Moments** window

For each section, tap on the button in the top left-hand corner to move back up to the previous level.

5 Tap on a photo within the **Moments** window to view it at full size

Double-tap with one finger on an individual photo to zoom in on it. Double-tap with one finger again to zoom back out. To zoom in to a greater degree, swipe outwards with thumb and forefinger.

6 Swipe with one finger or drag here to move through all of the available photos in a specific Moment

Don't forget

When photos are placed into albums the originals remain in the main **Photos** section. Any changes to the photos in the album will not affect the originals in Photos.

Creating Albums

Within the Photo app it is possible to create different albums in which you can store photos. This can be a good way to organize them according to different categories and headings. To do this:

1 Tap on the **Albums** button

Albums

2 Tap on this button

3 Enter a name for the new album

New Album
Enter a name for this album.

Madeira

Cancel   Save

4 Tap on the **Save** button

5 Tap on the photos you want to include in the album

Moments   Done
Add 7 photos to "Madeira".
Select

6 Tap on the **Done** button

Done

7 The new album is added to the Albums section in the Photos app

Madeira

Selecting Photos

It is easy to take hundreds, or thousands, of digital photos and most of the time you will only want to use a selection of them. Within the Photos app it is possible to select individual photos so that you can share them, delete them or add them to albums.

 Access the Moments section and tap on the **Select** button

Press and hold on a photo to access an option to copy it, rather than selecting it.

2 Tap on the photos you want to select, or tap on the **Select** button again to select all of the photos

To add items to an album, tap on this button in the **Moments** section.

3 Tap on the **Deselect** button if you want to remove the selection

Tap on photos to select them, then tap on the **Add To** button and select either an existing album or tap on the **New Album** link to create a new album with the selected photos added to it.

4 Use these buttons to, from left to right, share the selected photos, delete them or add them to an album

Photos Slideshow

All, or some, of your photos in the Photos app can be viewed in a continuous slideshow and you can even add your own music to it. To do this:

 Tap an **Album** to open it

 Tap the **Slideshow** button (if you can't see the controls, tap the screen)

 Drag the **Play Music** button **On** and tap on the **Music** button to select a song from the music library

 Tap on the **Transition** button to select an effect for when photos move from one to another

 Tap **Start Slideshow**. If you are showing the photos by connecting the iPad to a TV or AV projector use the Dissolve transition

6 Stop the slideshow by tapping the screen

Emailing Your Photos

You can email your photos to family, friends or work colleagues, directly from the Photos app. To do this:

 Open the **Photos** section by tapping on the relevant button at the bottom of the Photos app window

 Open a photo at full size, or tap on **Select** and tap on a photo to select it

 Tap the **Share** icon and choose **Mail**

4 Mail will open with the photo already added to the message

5 Compose the email and tap **Send**

...cont'd

Pasting a photo into an email

 Press and hold on a photo or image in **Photos**, web page or document

 Tap **Copy**

 Open **Mail** and select **New Message**

4 Press and hold inside the email body

5 Select **Paste** to paste the image into the email

Emailing multiple photos

1 Open a photo Album

2 Tap **Select**

 Select photos to email (up to five at a time)

4 Tap **Share** (top left) and choose **Mail**

5 The photos will be inserted into a blank email

Hot tip

You can paste photos into an email. You can even paste multiple photos into the same email.

Hot tip

iOS 8 makes it incredibly easy to share your pictures with Facebook, Twitter, etc. Tap the **Share** icon and choose the relevant social network. If you have not added an account you'll be prompted to do so.

Beware

You can only Share five pictures at a time using Mail. If you select more than five you will not see the Mail share option.

Adding Photos to Contacts

It's easy and more personal to assign a photograph to your contacts.

1 Open **Contacts**

2 Find the contact to which you want to add a photo

3 Tap **Edit** next to the person's name

4 Tap **Choose Photo**

5 You will be presented with a photo album and imported photos

6 Select the one you want to use

7 Move and scale until you're happy with the size and position

8 Tap **Use**

Personalize your contacts by adding photographs.

Alternative method

1 **Find a photo** and open it by tapping it

2 Tap the **Share** icon

3 Choose **Assign to Contact**

4 Choose the contact you want and voilà – the photo will be placed into the photo box for your contact

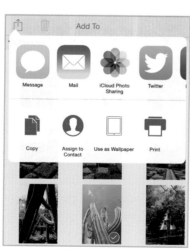

Taking Photos and Videos

Because of its mobility and the quality of the screen, the iPad is excellent for taking and displaying photos. Photos can be captured directly using one of the two built-in cameras (one on the front and one on the back) and then viewed, edited and shared using the Photos app. To do this:

 Tap on the **Camera** app

 Tap on this button to capture a photo (or press the volume button at the side of the iPad)

 Tap on this button to swap between the front or back cameras on the iPad

Tap on the HDR (High Dynamic Range) button to take three versions of the same subject that will then be blended into a single photo, using the best exposures from each photo.

The iPad cameras can be used for different formats:

TIME-LAPSE

VIDEO

• PHOTO

SQUARE

Swipe up or down at the side of the camera screen, underneath the shutter button, to access the different shooting options. Tap on the **Photo** button to capture photos at full screen size

Tap on the **Square** button to capture photos at this ratio

The iSight camera on the iPad Air 2 can also capture slow-motion video, with the Slo-Mo option.

 Tap on the **Time-lapse** button and press the shutter button (which appears red with ring around it) to create a time-lapse image: the camera keeps taking photos periodically until you press the shutter button again

 Tap on the **Video** button and press the red shutter button to take a video

Camera Settings

iCloud Sharing

Certain camera options can be applied within Settings. Several of these are to do with storing and sharing your photos via iCloud. To access these:

1 Tap on the **Settings** app

2 Tap on the **Photos & Camera** tab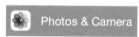

3 Drag the **iCloud Photo Library** button to **On** to
upload your whole photo library on your iPad to the iCloud (it remains on your iPad too). Similarly, photos on your other Apple devices can also be uploaded to the iCloud and these will be available on your iPad

4 Select an option for storing iCloud

| Optimize iPad Storage | ✓ |
| Download and Keep Originals | |

photos. (**Optimize iPad Storage** uses less storage as it uses device-optimized versions of your images, e.g. smaller file sizes

5 Drag the **Upload My Photo**

Upload to My Photo Stream ◯

Stream button to **On** to enable all new photos and videos that you take on your iPad to be uploaded automatically to the iCloud

6 Drag the **iCloud Photo Sharing** button to **On** to

iCloud Photo Sharing ◯

allow you to create albums within the Photos app that can then be shared with other people via iCloud

If the **iCloud Photo Library** option is **On** then your photos will all appear in the **All Photos** album in the Albums section, as well as in the Photos section. If iCloud Photo Library is **Off** there will be a **Camera Roll** album in the Albums section, where photos created on your iPad will appear.

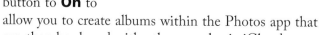

Drag the **Grid** button to On to place a grid over the screen when you are taking photos with the Camera, if required. This can be used to help compose photos by placing subjects using the grid.

Use Photos as Wallpaper

Wallpaper, as well as being something you paste onto the walls of your house, is also the term for the backdrop used for the iPad screens. Apple has produced some gorgeous wallpapers for you to use but you can use your own images if you prefer.

 Find the photo you want to use in **Photos**

 Tap to open the picture at full size

 Tap the **Share** icon

 Tap **Use as Wallpaper**

You will then have the option to use this for the Lock Screen or Wallpaper or both.

Hot tip

You can use your own photos as wallpapers.

7 Videos

The iPad, with its Retina Display, is ideal for video. The high resolution screen and ease of use make Videos a perfect app for watching movies you have bought through iTunes or converted from your own DVDs. You can also record video using the iPad's in-built cameras.

Getting Video onto the iPad

The iPad is a great multimedia device for watching movies, TV shows, video podcasts and other video content. The resolution of the screen makes movies crisp and clear. On the iPad, movies can be downloaded and viewed by using the **Videos** app.

Different ways to get videos onto the iPad

- Buy or rent videos using iTunes on the iPad or computer

- Sync videos from the Mac or PC using iTunes

- Using email if the video is short

- Using iPhoto on the Mac (use the Photos pane in iTunes)

- From a folder on your hard drive

Getting your own DVDs onto the iPad

You may have purchased (physical) DVDs and would like to watch them on your iPad. But how can you get them on the iPad? There are several programs for both PC and Mac that will convert DVDs into a variety of formats including iPhone, Apple TV, iPad, and many other formats. Handbrake (**http://handbrake.fr)** is a free app available for both Mac and Windows platforms that makes the conversion so easy.

Hot tip

Use Handbrake to convert your own DVDs for the iPad.

Handbrake has an iPad option at present but I use *AppleTV* which looks great on the iPad and Apple TV.

Playing Videos

To play videos on the iPad you need to open the **Videos** app.

 Tap **Videos** to open the app. Click on the **Store** button

 Tap the **Category** you want to watch, e.g. **Movies**

 Select the one you want

If the video has chapters you can choose a specific chapter to watch.

Where are the controls?

You can use the scrubber bar to move forwards and backwards to a specific place in the video.

 Tap the **iPad screen** while the movie is playing

 The controls (**scrubber bar** and **volume**) will appear on screen

 Slide the **playhead** (filled circle) to where you want to view

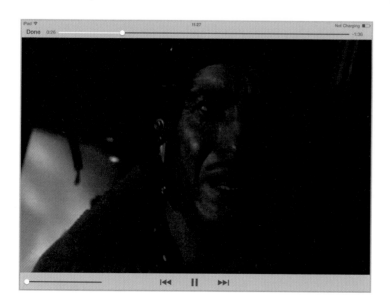

...cont'd

The video controls are fairly standard, and are similar throughout iPad apps that play video, including YouTube. The main ones to note in Videos are those that make the screen fill or fit the page. As well as tapping the icons, you can make the video fill the screen by double-tapping the screen while the movie is playing. Double-tapping again will make the video fit (not fill) the screen.

Hot tip

Tap the screen twice when a movie is playing to make it fill the screen. Tap twice again to make it fit the screen.

Pause video	Tap here to pause	❚❚
Resume playing	Tap here or press center button on Apple headset	▶
Increase/decrease volume	Drag volume slider control or use buttons on Apple headset	
Start video over	Tap the playhead all the way to the LEFT or tap here	◄◄
Skip to next chapter (if video contains chapters)	Tap here or press the center button twice on Apple headset	►►❙
Skip to previous chapter	Tap here or press the center button three times on Apple headset	❙◄◄
Start playback at specific chapter	Tap chapter icon then select the chapter you want to view	
Fast forward/Rewind	Touch and hold these buttons	►►❙ ❙◄◄
Move to specific point in video	Drag playhead to desired point	
Stop watching movie before the end	Tap **Done** or the Home button to quit the Videos app	
Scale video to fill or fit screen	Tap here to fill screen	↖ ↘
	Tap here to fit the screen	↘ ↖

Purchased or Rented Movies

You can rent or buy movies from the iTunes Store. Also, if you have purchased movies using Apple TV these can be synced to your iPad.

 1 Rent or buy movies from the iTunes Store. Allow the movie to download completely (you cannot watch the movie until it has fully downloaded)

 2 Tap **Videos** app

 3 Tap **Movies**

 **4** Tap the movie you want to watch

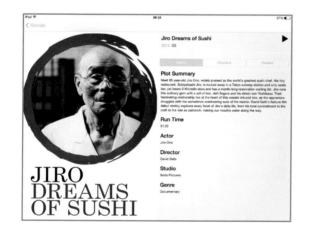

Sync movies purchased on Mac, PC or Apple TV

 1 Connect iPad to computer

2 Go to **iPad > Movies** pane in iTunes and check the movie(s) you want to sync to the iPad

 3 Click **Apply** then **Sync Now**

Note: The movies you rent *directly* on the iPad cannot be transferred to your computer.

Movies rented on the iPad cannot be transferred to your computer.

Some music CDs have music videos included, or you may buy Music videos on Apple TV or from another source. These should show up in a separate section of Movies (Music Videos).

Removing Videos from iPad

Several ways of taking movies off your iPad

 Tap **Videos** on the iPad Home Screen to open the app

 Tap and hold the movie you want to remove

3 The **Delete** button will appear

4 Tap the **X** icon to delete the movie

Remove a movie using iTunes

Hot tip

If you delete a movie on the iPad you will still have a copy on your computer which you can use to resync the movie back to your iPad.

1 With the iPad connected to your computer

2 Go to **iTunes > Movies**

3 **Deselect** the movie you want to remove from the iPad

 Click **Apply** then **Sync**

The selected movie will be removed from the iPad. The movie will *remain* on your computer and if you want to sync it back to the iPad, check its radio button in iTunes.

Watch Movies on TV or Screen

You can connect your iPad to a TV or AV projector. You will need to buy an Apple Lightning to VGA Adapter or a Lightning Digital AV Adapter (for HDMI).

Apple iPad dock to VGA Adapter

Apple Digital AV Adapter (allows HDMI output and charging of iPad at the same time)

Hot tip

If you have Apple TV 2 or later you can share your videos using AirPlay wirelessly.

1 **Connect the iPad** to the TV

2 **Select PC** option using your TV's input controls

3 Tap **Videos** to open the app, then select the movie you want to watch

Beware

You cannot play DRM movies on the TV or a screen using the VGA Connector.

Not all movies can be played
Some movies will not play through the TV – those with DRM (Digital Rights Management) may not play and you may see a warning that you are not authorized to play the movie. The solution (though expensive) may be to buy the movie on physical DVD then run it through Handbrake using the Universal Option, and this should play fine through the TV.

Recording and Editing Video

Recording videos using the iPad is as easy as taking still pictures. Once recorded, you can edit your video and trim unwanted footage, email or send your video to iCloud or YouTube, or share your video by sending to Apple TV.

1 Tap on the **Camera** app

2 Swipe up or down so that the **Video** button is highlighted

3 Tap on this button to swap cameras from front to back

4 Tap on this button to record a video. Tap on it again to stop recording

5 Once a video has been captured it is saved within the **Photos** app with the video camera icon and the duration of the video showing on the thumbnail

126

The iSight camera on the iPad Air 2 can also capture slow-motion video, with the Slo-Mo option.

6 Tap on this button in the middle of the screen to play a video

7 Tap on this button to share a video through the standard iPad options and also social networking sites such as YouTube and Facebook (if you have accounts with these services)

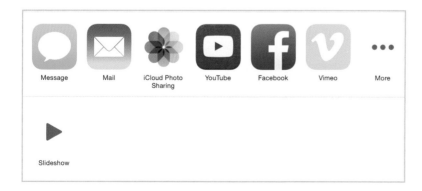

Hot tip

To share your video on Facebook, go to your Facebook page via the Facebook app or the Facebook site (**www. facebook.com**) and follow instructions to upload videos.

127

...cont'd

Editing videos

You cannot edit videos with the Photos app but there is a range of apps in the App Store that can be downloaded and used to edit your own videos.

iMovie

This is the iPad version of the Apple video editing app and offers a wide range of editing options and effects.

Finding apps

Access the App Store and enter **video editing** into the Search box to find a wider range of this type of app.

8 Podcasts

Instead of storing podcasts in the Music *app, iOS 8 can use an app specially designed like the* App Store *and* iBooks *where you can browse and subscribe to podcasts. The* Podcasts *app doubles as a podcast audio and video player. It comes preinstalled with iOS 8.*

The Podcasts App

Podcasts are audio or video broadcasts that can be created by individuals or taken from programs that have been broadcast, usually on the radio. In iOS 8, the podcasts app is one of the preinstalled ones and can be used to download podcasts:

Podcasts can no longer be stored and accessed from the Music app.

Open the Podcasts app

These are the podcasts I subscribe to and have chosen to sync to the iPad. The number of unplayed episodes is shown in the red circles at the top right of the podcast icon. I can change this view to a list view (*shown on the next page*).

Subscribed podcasts in list view

Tap on a podcast to start playing it:

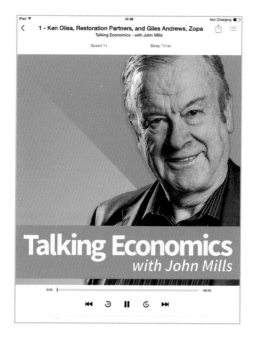

Finding Podcasts

You can search for podcasts from within the Podcasts app.

Using the Podcasts app to find new podcasts

Swipe up and down the screen to view the range of podcasts:

Using Top Charts

A cool feature of the Podcasts app is Top Charts. Almost like using a radio, you can dial up a category and top podcasts in that category are shown.

Here are audio (note audio/video icons at the top) podcasts in the TV & Film category.

Now we are in the Health, Fitness & Nutrition category. Again, this is an audio rather than video podcast.

Listening to Podcasts

If you play an audio podcast you hear only sound, while video podcasts play movie podcasts.

This **Learning Guitar Now** podcast is a video podcast, showing all the usual video controls similar to the Videos app.

This **CoffeeBreak Spanish** podcast is an audio podcast.

9 Calendar

You can never be too organized!

Calendar makes it easy to set up all of

your appointments and also store and

share them using iCloud.

Calendar Navigation

The Calendar app has a clear layout and interface, making it easy to enter and edit appointments. The app is designed to resemble a physical calendar, with a left and right page. Each shows different items depending on which view you are using.

In the **Day** view, the left column shows that day's appointments, with the whole day spread out on the right. The **Week** view shows the whole seven days with all appointments clearly labeled. The **Month** view shows the whole month's appointments, and the **List** view shows both right and left pages with the current day on the right and the list of all appointments (the total Calendar appointments) in the left column. The example below is Day view.

Hot tip

You don't need to open the app to see the date – it shows on the app's icon even if it hasn't been opened, just like Calendar on the Mac.

View by Day, Week, Month or Year   Search Add Event

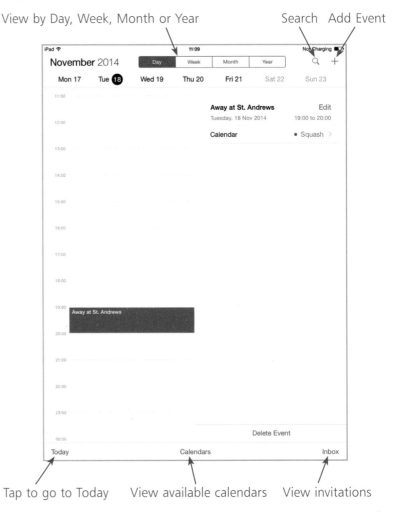

Tap to go to Today   View available calendars   View invitations

The Calendar Views

You can look at your calendar using **Day**, **Week**, **Month**, or **Year** views.

Week view showing detailed information for each day

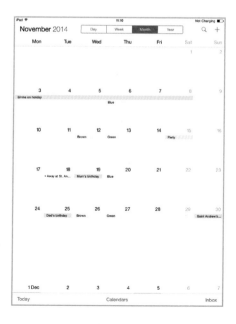

Month view

In Month view, you can scroll continuously through the calendar. This means that you do not have to just view a single month on its own, you can view the end of one month and the beginning of the next month in the same calendar window.

Adding Events

You can add events (e.g. *appointments*) to Calendar directly on the iPad. If the Calendar is turned on for iCloud, everything within the app will be available via iCloud and any compatible iCloud devices which also have the Calendar app.

To add appointments directly onto the iPad

 Open the **Calendar** app

 Tap **+** at the top right of the Calendar window or press and hold on a specific date

 Enter a title for the event in the **Title** field

 Enter a location if necessary in the **Location** field

5 Drag the **All-day** button to **Off**. Tap **Starts** and rotate dials to the required start time

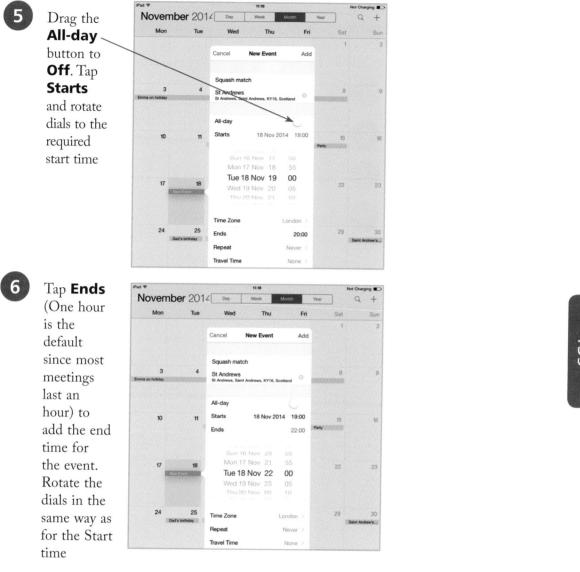

6 Tap **Ends** (One hour is the default since most meetings last an hour) to add the end time for the event. Rotate the dials in the same way as for the Start time

7 Tap **Repeat** if you want to repeat the event, e.g. anniversary, birthday

8 If you want a reminder tap **Alert**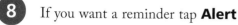

9 Tap **Calendar** to assign the event to a specific calendar if you have more than one

Editing Calendar Events

This is very straightforward. Again, you can edit in your computer calendar program or edit directly on the iPad using any of the views (Day, Week, Month or List). Tapping the appointment once in Day or List view takes you straight into edit mode.

 Tap the **event** to open it

 Tap **Edit**

 Amend the event, making your changes

 Tap **Done**

Deleting Events

You can delete appointments using your computer or using the iPad. Either way, it's pretty simple.

 Tap **Calendar** and open the event by tapping it once then tapping **Edit**

 At the bottom of the pop-up you will see **Delete Event**

3 Tap **Delete Event** to delete at the bottom of the Edit window

Calendar Alarms

How can you be sure you don't miss a crucial appointment? You could look at the Calendar app daily or more often and scan through upcoming events.

But an easier way is to set an alarm, or reminder if the event is really important, for example you might want a reminder two days before an assignment has to be handed in.

On the iPad Calendar, reminders appear as notifications (with sound) on the screen. Set these up by going to **Edit** mode then tap **Alert**. Decide how far ahead you want the alert.

The alert shows as a notification on the screen (locked or unlocked), at the allocated time, and there will be an alarm sound so you cannot ignore the alert.

10 Contacts

Gone are the days when we stored contacts just on a cell phone SIM card. The world of contacts has become much more advanced and Contacts *makes it easy to add and view contacts, making their details instantly available on your iPad.*

Exploring the Contacts App

The Contacts app is a simple but elegant app for managing all of your contact information. The app is designed to resemble a physical address book, showing your **Contacts** and **Groups** down the left hand page with contact details shown on the right facing page.

Groups button   Search box   Add a new contact   Edit contact

iPad 📶   10:12   ⚡ Not Charging 🔋

Groups   **All Contacts**   +   Edit

🔍 Search

T
Pat Tulloy

Euan **Turner**

V

Robin **V**   A

Eildih **Vandome**   B
                                              C
Lucy **Vandome**   D
                                              E
Mark **Vandome**   F
                                              G
Mike **Vandome**   H
                                              I
Nick **Vandome**   J
                                              K
Peter **Vandome**   L
                                              M
Robin **Vandome**   N
Wendy **Vandome**   O
                                              P
Vhairi   Q
W   R
                                              S
Clare **Wallace**   T
                                              U
Isobel **Walton**   V
                                              W
Jim **Watson**   X
                                              Y
David **Watt**   Z
                                              #
Jim **Westcott**

Claire **White**

John **Willan**

DAVID **WILLIAMS**

Nick Vandome
"Nick"
Nick Vandome

mobile
07891 123456   💬

FaceTime   📹 📞

home
nickvandome@mac.com   ✉️ 💬

home
1 High Street
Perth
United Kingdom

Game Center
{ Nick729 }

Notes

Send Message

Share Contact

Alphabetical thumb tabs   Share contact details

You can also browse Contacts in landscape view but the details are much the same as portrait although the pages are a bit wider.

Tap on a contact in the left-hand panel to view their details in the right-hand panel.

iPad 🛜		10:12		⚡ Not Charging 🔋
Groups **All Contacts** +				Edit

Q Search

T
~~Pat Talley~~

Euan **Turner**

V

Robin **V**

Eildih **Vandome**

Lucy **Vandome**

Mark **Vandome**

Mike **Vandome**

Nick **Vandome**

Peter **Vandome**

Nick Vandome
"Nick"
Nick Vandome

mobile
07891 123456

FaceTime

home
nickvandome@mac.com

home
1 High Street
Perth
United Kingdom

Game Center
{ Nick729 }

Toggle between Groups and All Contacts

If you have groups, you can access these from within Contacts. Although you can add to a group, you cannot set up a group on Contacts – the group itself needs to be created using your computer contacts app. To view your groups:

1 Tap the **Groups** button to view all groups

iPad 🛜	
Groups	**All Contacts**

2 Tap a group name to select it and tap on the **Done** button to view the members in the group

iPad		
	Groups	Done
ICLOUD		
All Contacts		
P3 Squash		✓
Work		

Beware

You cannot create new groups in the Contacts app; you can only add to existing ones.

Adding Contacts

You can add contacts directly onto the iPad (these will sync later to your computer).

To add a new contact:

1   Launch **Contacts**

2   Tap the **+** icon at the bottom of the left hand page

3   Enter details into Contact page, adding a photo if necessary

4   Click **Done** when finished

Adding to Groups

With the Contacts app you can also view groups of people for areas such as hobbies, family or work. To do this:

1 Launch **Contacts** and tap the **Groups** button to view all groups

iPad		
Groups	All Contacts	+

2 Tap a group name to select it

3 Tap **Done** to view the contents of the group

iPad		
	Groups	Done
ICLOUD		
All Contacts		
P3 Squash		✓
Work		

4 Tap the **+** button to create a new entry for the group

iPad		
Groups	**Contacts**	+
Q Search		
B		A
Geoff **Bush**		B
F		C
		D
Richard **Frenz**		E
G		F
		G
John **Gillespie**		H
H		I
Stuart **Hunter**		J

5 Enter the details for the new entry (the entry will be added to the group and also All Contacts in the Contacts app)

08:18		87% ▮
Cancel	**New Contact**	Done
add photo	Colin	
	Smith	⊗
	Company	
⊕ add phone		

6 Tap **Done**

7 Tap the **Groups** button and tap on **All Contacts** to view everyone in your contacts. Tap **Done** to view your contacts

iPad		
	Groups	Done
ICLOUD		
All Contacts		✓
P3 Squash		✓
Work		✓

Beware

On the iPad, groups in the Contacts app cannot be used to send a group email to the members of the group. However, on a Mac computer the group name can be entered into the **To** box of an email and all of the members will be inserted, using the details from the Contacts app.

Edit and Delete Contacts

Edit a contact

This is easy and can be done on the computer (changes will sync later) or directly on the iPad.

1 Open the **Contacts** app

2 Select the contact and tap on **Edit**

3 Amend the details

4 Tap **Done** when finished

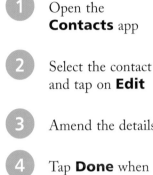

Delete a contact

You can delete contacts by removing them from Calendar, or Microsoft Outlook on your Mac or PC, and when you next sync, that contact will be removed.

Or you can delete straight from the iPad itself.

1 Open the **Contacts** app

2 Select the contact you want to delete

3 Tap **Edit**

4 Scroll to the bottom of the contact page

5 Tap **Delete Contact**

Assigning Photos

You won't want to have photos for all your contacts but for family and friends it is great to have their picture displayed in the contact list.

1 Open **Contacts**

2 Find the contact to which you want to assign a photo

3 Tap **Edit** and tap on **add photo** next to their name

4 Tap **Choose Photo**

5 Select a photo from those stored on your iPad

6 Tap **Use** or **Choose** when you are happy with your choice of photo

Add photos to friends' and family contacts – it makes it more personal.

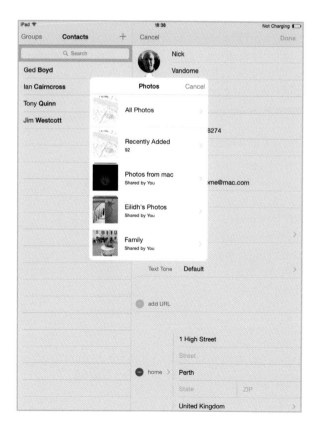

Sharing Contact Details

You can send a contact's details to a friend using email.

 Open the **Contacts** app

 Select the contact you want to share

 Tap **Share Contact** underneath their details and select an option for sharing, such as **Message** or **Mail**

Send an iMessage to a Contact

Apple introduced iMessage for iPhone and iPad, and now OS X for Mac. Using your iPad you can send an iMessage if you are on Wi-Fi or cellular network. If you use an iPhone you can send iMessages or SMS but the iPad only has the iMessage option.

 Open the **Messages** app

 Tap the **+** button in the **To:** box and enter a contact to message and choose their email/phone number

Type your text and add a photo, if required, (icon to the left of the message box) then tap **Send**

11 Notes

Notes *takes the place of post-its. The app is simple but effective. Not only can you make and store notes on your iPad, you can also sync these using iCloud so you need never forget anything again.*

What is the Notes App?

Notes is one of the simplest and most effective of the preinstalled apps. Like several other Apple apps it also operates with iCloud. It resembles a blank notepad. What you see depends on whether you hold the iPad in the portrait or landscape position.

In portrait mode (right) you can see all notes in a floating window. The landscape mode (below) is more impressive, with a list of notes in the left-hand panel, with the current note being viewed on the right.

Each time a note is edited it goes back to the top of the list in the left-hand panel.

152

Syncing notes

Notes can be created and stored only on your iPad, or they can be stored in the iCloud so that they are not only backed up, but also available on other devices.

Adding a New Note

When a new note is created it appears at the top of the list of notes, in the left-hand panel, as shown in the bottom image on the previous page. To create a new note:

 Tap this symbol at the upper right of the screen

 A new note is generated

 Type in your text (on the first line, enter something that tells you what the note is about since the first line is used as the title of the note)

4 To finish, tap **Notes** (upper left corner of the window) to take you back to the list of notes

5 Your new note will now be in the list with the date on which it was created, or updated, above it

Sharing Notes

As well as viewing your notes on the iPad, you can email them to yourself and to others. You can also send the note in a Message, as well as copy and print the note.

1 Open the **Notes** app

2 Add a new note or open an existing note

3 Tap the **Share** icon at the top of the screen and select the **Mail** option

4 A new email window will open and the cursor will be flashing in the **To:** field

5 Enter the address of the recipient

6 Tap **Send**

Note sharing options
Notes can also be shared directly from the app. To do this:

1 Tap the Share icon and select one of the sharing options (you can also copy and print the note from here)

Message Mail Twitter Facebook

Copy Print More

Notes Accounts and iCloud

Notes can be created to be shared via iCloud, or just created and kept on your iPad. In general, it is better to store them in the iCloud as this then makes them available via other iCloud-enabled devices and you can also be reassured that they are being stored and backed up online. To use Notes in iCloud:

1 If iCloud is turned off for Notes, there are no account options and the notes are only stored on your iPad

iPad 🛜		15:42
iPad iOS 8	15:35	31 July 2014 15:35
		iPad iOS 8

2 Access the Settings app and tap on the **iCloud** link

iCloud
nickvandome@mac.com

3 Drag the **Notes** button to **On**

Notes

4 If Notes is turned **On** in iCloud there will be **Accounts** link at the top of the notes list. Tap on this to view the available accounts

❮ Accounts

iPad iOS 8	**16:38**
Books 2014	**16:37**

...cont'd

5 The accounts are listed. They are for **All Notes, On My iPad** and **iCloud**

iPad 📶

Accounts

All Notes   >

ON MY IPAD

Notes   >

ICLOUD

All iCloud   >

New Folder   >

New Folder 2   >

New Folder 3   >

Notes   >

Recovered Items   >

Beware

New folders within iCloud can only be created and renamed within the Notes app on a Mac computer.

Don't forget

Notes cannot be moved once they have been created in a folder.

6 Tap on a folder to view the items within it. In some cases this may be blank, e.g. if all of your notes are stored in the iCloud and you tap on the On My iPad folder. Tap on the **Accounts** button to go back to the main Accounts panel

❮ Accounts

No Notes

(12) Maps

Maps *makes it easy to identify your location, wherever you are, find places, gauge traffic conditions and get directions to anywhere – on foot, by car and using apps for public transport.*

What is Maps?

If you have an iPhone you will be familiar with Maps since the iPad version is pretty similar although much enhanced. The app shows you a map of where you are, what direction you are facing, street names, directions to a given place from where you are currently (walking, by car and by public transport), and traffic.

The iPad version's large screen shows several views:

- Standard

- Satellite

- Hybrid

- 2D or 3D

To use Maps you will need an active Internet connection – either Wi-Fi or cellular.

Beware

You need an active network connection to use Maps to its full capabilities.

The Maps Views

There are four views, each showing slightly different detail. Standard is probably the most useful since it shows the typical style of map layout.

The different views can be accessed by tapping on the **i** symbol in the bottom right-hand corner of the screen.

Standard view – stylistic but very functional

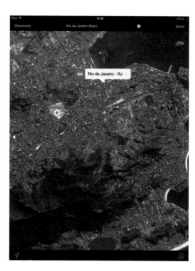

Satellite view – as the name suggests is a satellite image of the area

Hybrid view – combines the satellite detail with street names overlaid

Satellite 3D view – showing parks, water and other terrain

Although less glitzy, the Standard view is the most practical in a lot of cases.

Finding Places

You can find a location using a number of methods

- Address
- By intersection
- Area
- Landmark
- Bookmark
- Contact
- ZIP/postal code

Hot tip

Maps has the ability to show you places of interest.

To find a location

1 Tap the **Search field** to show the keyboard

2 Enter the address or other search information

3 Tap **Search** on the keyboard

4 A pin will drop onto the map showing location

5 Maps will display places of interest nearby

Zoom in and out

Zoom in	Pinch map with thumb and forefinger and spread apart or double-tap with one finger to zoom in
Zoom out	Pinch map with thumb and forefinger and bring together or tap with two fingers to zoom out
Pan and scroll	Drag the map up, down, left or right

Your Current Location

Find your current location

 Tap on this button

 A compass will show the direction you are facing

 Your **location** is shown as a blue marker

The digital compass

 Compass icon, but compass is white which means it is not active

 Tap the compass icon and it turns blue and now shows North

 Tap again and this icon points to show you the direction you are facing

Hot tip

Tap the compass to find out which direction you are facing. May save you having to do a U-turn!

161

Want to know more about your current location?

 Tap the **blue/gray button**

Current Location >

 Tap the (**i**) symbol

 Details of your location will be displayed

1D Young Street

Address
Current Location

Popular Apps Nearby

Create New Contact

Add to Existing Contact

Report a Problem

Marking Locations

How to mark locations

You can drop pins onto the map for future reference.

 1 Touch and hold any location to drop a pin

 2 Touch and hold then **drag the pin** to the desired location

 3 To save it, tap the Share button and then tap **Add to Favorites**

4 That pin will serve as a marker for future use

5 To see your dropped pin locations tap **Bookmarks**

6 A list of your dropped pins will appear

7 Tap the one you want to view

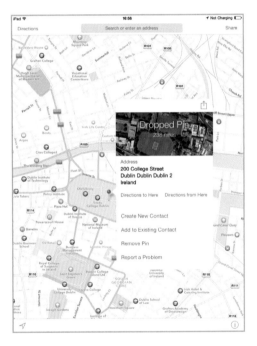

Hot tip

Marking locations is very easy – just touch and hold your finger on the screen to drop a pin.

Edit your bookmarks

Just like a web browser, you can edit and delete the bookmarked locations.

Clear bookmarks

Tap **Edit** then tap the delete symbol.

Using Flyover Tour

One of the innovative features in the Maps app in iOS 8 is the Flyover Tour function. This is an animated Flyover Tour of certain location that gives you a 3D tour of a city in Satellite view. To view a Flyover Tour:

 1 If the Flyover Tour function is available for the location you are viewing there will be a **3D Flyover Tour** option. Tap on this to start the Flyover Tour (from any map view)

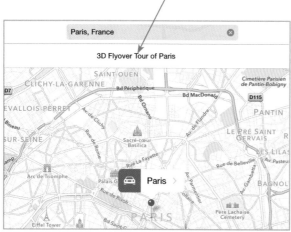

The Flyover Tour function is only available for certain cities around the world, with the majority being in the USA. This is currently over 60, with more being added steadily.

2 The tour starts and takes you through an aerial 3D tour of the main sights of the location

When viewing maps, the compass icon in the top right-hand corner indicates the direction of north.

3 The tour will end automatically, or you can tap on the **End Flyover Tour** button at any time

End Flyover Tour

Get Directions

Directions are available for driving, public transport, and walking

 Tap **Directions**

 Enter the **Start** and **End** locations into the boxes at the top of the screen

 If the address is in the **Contacts** list tap and choose the contact

 Tap this icon if you want to reverse the directions

 Choose **Directions** for driving, or walking, or apps for taking public transport

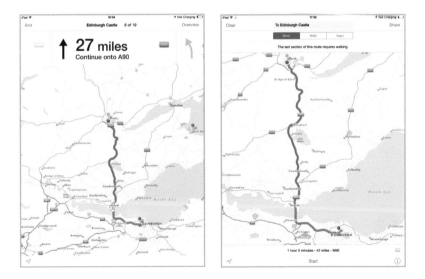

You can view the directions as an overview or a stepwise guide by tapping on the **Start** button

...cont'd

Alternative method for finding directions

 Tap a **pin** on the map

 Tap **Directions to Here** or **Directions from Here**

 Reverse by tapping this button

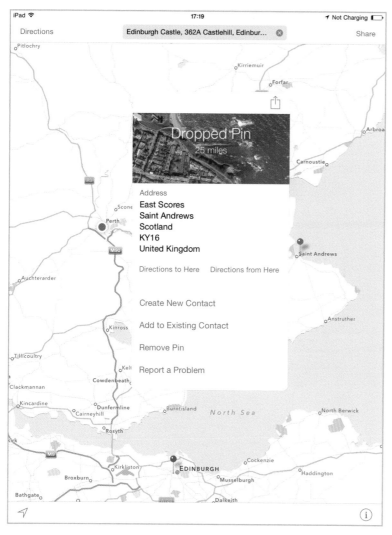

Traffic Conditions

Maps can show you the traffic conditions for locations.
(This feature did not work for all countries or cities at the time of printing.)

 Tap the **i** symbol in the bottom right-hand corner of the screen to view the map options and tap on the **Show Traffic** button

 The traffic conditions are shown as colors:

Green	average speed is >50mph
Yellow	25-50mph
Red	<25mph
Gray	traffic information is not available

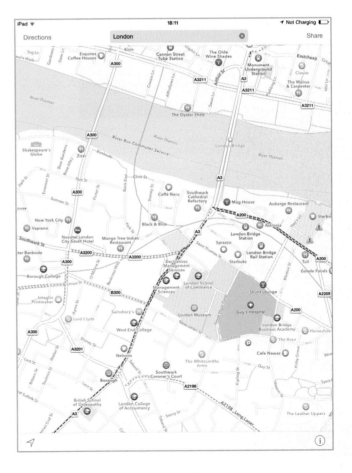

13 Music

The original iPod revolutionized the way we store and listen to music and other audio content. The iPad's Music app continues this tradition and is a great music player, and much more.

The Music Interface

This is similar to the standard Music interface on the iPod and iPhone but because the screen is so much larger, the app is clearer and easier to use. You can browse your music by *Artist, Album, Song* and several other ways. Although the iPad has an internal speaker, the music quality is not top quality. You need to attach a decent pair of headphones to hear the full quality of the Music app sound.

Music

Music can also be played with the iTunes Radio service (*only available in the US and Australia at the time of printing*).

iPad 🔋	11:21	🔋 25%

0:00 | -3:05

⏮ ▶ ⏭ The Beatles **Here Comes the Sun** Abbey   Repeat   Shuffle

Store	**Songs**	Now Playing ›

Shuffle   ✕

A

Absent Friends	The Divine Comedy	Absent Friends - Single
Absolute Beginners	David Bowie	The Singles Collection
After the Storm	Mumford & Sons	Sigh No More
Another One Bites the D...	Queen	The Platinum Collectio...
Another One Bites the D...	Queen & Wyclef Jean	The Platinum Collectio...
Ashes to Ashes	David Bowie	The Singles Collection
Atomic	Blondie	Blondie: Greatest Hits
Awake My Soul	Mumford & Sons	Sigh No More
Awake My Soul	Mumford & Sons	Sigh No More

B

Barcelona	Queen & Montserrat Ca...	The Platinum Collectio...
Battery Kinzie	Fleet Foxes	Helplessness Blues
Beauty and the Beast	David Bowie	The Singles Collection
Beauty and the Beast	David Bowie	The Singles Collection

Q A B C D E F G H I J K L M N O P Q R S T U V W X Y Z #

Playlists	Artists	Songs	Albums	Genres	Compilations	Composers

By using the buttons at the bottom of the screen you can browse through your music in a number of ways, including by Artist, Song, Album, Genre or Composer.

Browsing your library by Songs – Playlists are shown in the left panel, and all the songs on your iPad are shown on the right

Browsing the iPad by Albums – you can see the cover art clearly

If you have created playlists you can tap Playlists and select the one you want

The Composer view – probably the least useful of all the views. Looks much like Artist view

Music Controls

The Music controls can be accessed from the library window or when you tap the cover art for the current track.

The controls are very intuitive and are much the same as for the standard iPod. If the controls are not obvious, you may need to tap the screen to bring them up (the same is true of most apps – when video or music content is playing on the iPad, the controls fade).

The main controls used to play music are shown below. What you see varies depending on how you are browsing your music.

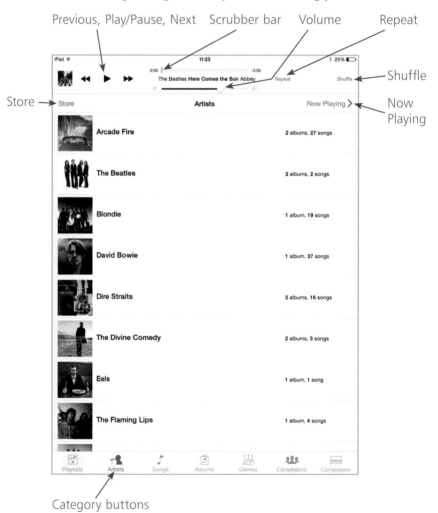

Previous, Play/Pause, Next · Scrubber bar · Volume · Repeat · Shuffle · Store · Now Playing · Category buttons

Playing Music

Once music has been bought on iTunes it can be played on your iPad using the Music app. To do this:

1   Tap on the **Music** app

2   Use these buttons to find songs by different criteria

3   Tap on a track to select it and start it playing

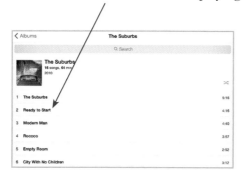

4   Tap on the middle button to pause/play a selected song

5   Drag this button to increase or decrease the volume

6   Tap on this button to **Repeat** a song or album after it has played

7   Tap on this button to **Shuffle** the order of songs

Hot tip

To create a Playlist of songs, tap on the **Playlists** button, then tap on the **New** button. Give it a name and then add songs from your Library.

Hot tip

Music controls, including Play, Fast Forward, Rewind and Volume can also be applied in the **Control Center**, which can be accessed by swiping up from the bottom of the screen.

iTunes Store

This is covered in more detail in Chapter 14.

From the Music app, tap **Store** (top left in the Music window) and you will be taken straight to the store (you will be taken out of the Music app to the iTunes Store, which is a separate app).

Here you can browse available content which includes:

- Music
- Films
- TV programmes
- Audiobooks
- Top Charts
- Genius
- Purchased (items you have purchased previously)

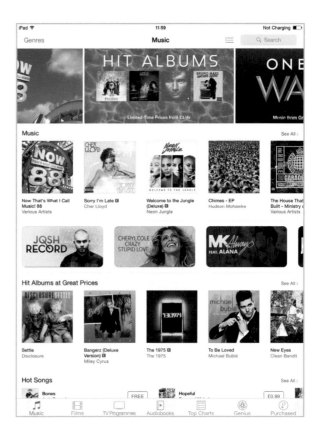

Buying Music

Music on the iPad can be downloaded and played using the iTunes and the Music apps respectively. iTunes links to the iTunes Store, from where music, and other content, can be bought and downloaded to your iPad. To do this:

 1 Tap on the **iTunes Store** app

 2 Tap on the **Music** button on the iTunes toolbar at the bottom of the window

3 Tap on an item to view it. Tap here to buy an album or tap on the button next to a song to buy that individual item

Beware

You need to have an Apple ID with credit or debit card details added to be able to buy music from the iTunes Store.

 4 Purchased items are included in the Music app's Library

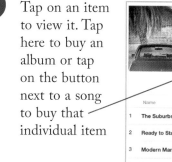

Creating Playlists

This is a great way to collect songs you like into one list rather than having to hunt around for them.

Hot tip

Creating playlists is the easiest way to group your favorite tracks together.

 Tap on the **Playlists** button on the bottom toolbar and tap on the **New Playlist** button (towards the top, left of the Music screen)

 Enter a **Name** for your playlist then tap **Save**

 All of your songs on the iPad will be listed

 Click (**+**) for each one you want to add

 When added, the track listing turns gray so you know it has been added to the playlist

 When you are happy with the selection tap **Done**

7 To edit the playlist, select it and tap **Edit** and remove/add other songs, or change the playing order by moving tracks up and down (touch and hold the track with your finger then move the track)

Name the playlist and tap **Save**   Add the tracks you want

14 iTunes Store

The iTunes Store is a huge resource for music, movies, TV shows, audiobooks and other media. The iPad version is simple to use so you can browse the iTunes Store and download content quickly and easily.

Welcome to the iTunes Store

This app is a great hub for browsing new music, and renting or buying music and other media including:

- Songs and albums
- Videos
- TV shows
- Audiobooks

There are more than 20 million music tracks and thousands of movies available for download. Purchases can be made using your iTunes account or redeeming an iTunes gift card.

You will need an iTunes account to buy things from the Store, and for many functions on the iPad. If you haven't got one it would be best to set one up.

First, log in to your iTunes account

1. Tap **Settings**
2. Tap **Store**
3. Tap **Sign In**
4. Enter your **username** and **password**

If you don't have an iTunes account

1. Tap **Settings**
2. Tap **Store**
3. Tap **Create New Account**
4. Follow the instructions to lead you through the setup process

Hot tip

The iTunes Store has >28 million music tracks, >1 million podcasts, and >45,000 movies.

Beware

You need an iTunes account to use the iTunes Store. If you don't have one, set one up!

Hot tip

An extensive range of educational material can also be accessed from the iTunes U app, which can be downloaded from the App Store.

Layout of the iTunes Store

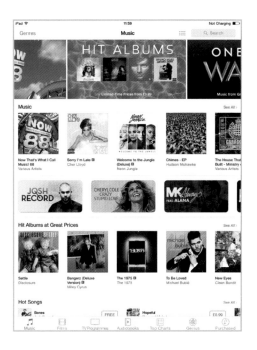

Finding content using Genres

Tap on the **More** button on the top toolbar to view the full range of **Categories**.

Music

Browse music by tapping the **Music** icon at the bottom of the iTunes Store screen.

You can browse:

- All Genres

- Pop

- Dance

- Alternative (when viewed in landscape mode)

- More Categories

Tap on the **Genius** button at the bottom of the screen to view recommendations based on previous purchases.

Hot tip

Genius is a great way of finding new music.

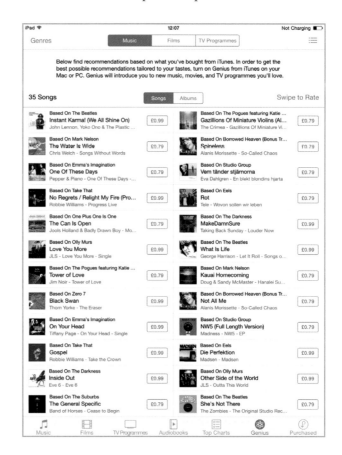

Movies

The store makes it easy to browse for movies and to rent or buy these. You can browse by All Genres, Action & Adventure, Classics, Comedy and More Categories.

Previewing movie information

 Tap the **movie** to open an information window which shows the cost of rental or purchase

 Select standard definition (SD) or high definition (HD)

 Tap the **Trailer** image to see a short preview of the film before you buy

4 Tap the **Share** icon to send a link to the movie by email or message, or upload to Twitter or Facebook. You can also **Gift** the movie to a friend

High definition versions of movies are usually more expensive to rent or buy than the standard definition versions.

TV Shows

Just like Movies, you can buy or rent TV Shows directly from the iTunes Store.

Browse by:

- All Genres

- Animation

- Comedy

- Drama (when viewed in landscape mode)

- More Categories

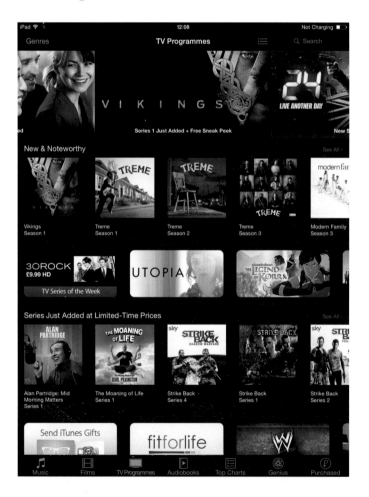

Audiobooks

As the name suggests, audiobooks are books which are listened to rather than read. These are ideal for people who have visual problems.

There are many titles available in the iTunes Store but there are many other sites listing free and paid audiobooks for downloading to your iPad:

- **http://www.audible.co.uk**

- **http://www.audiobooks.org**

- **http://librivox.org**

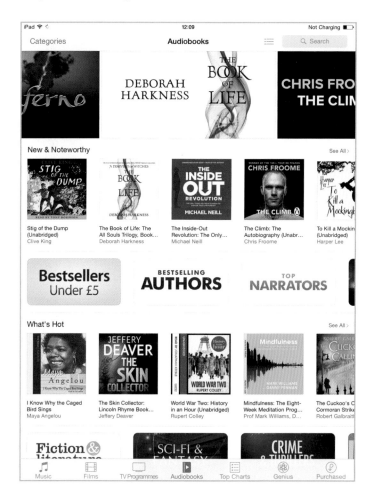

Genius Suggestions

If you are stuck for ideas for what to buy in terms of music, films, or TV shows you can let Genius make suggestions for you. Genius will look at your previous purchases and make suggestions for you. If you have never bought a TV program using iTunes Store it will say *You do not currently have any recommendations in this category.*

To see the Genius suggestions tap the Genius button at the bottom of the iTunes Store page and select a category at the top.

Above you can see items that Genius has suggested I might buy, based on previous purchases.

15 The App Store

The Apps store is a vast repository of apps for the iPhone and iPad. The number of third-party apps grows by the day. You can browse and purchase from this burgeoning store right from your iPad and increase its capabilities by adding additional functionality.

App Store Layout

The App Store is Apple's online store for users of iOS devices to review and download apps for almost any activity imaginable. Some apps are free, while others have to be paid for.

At the time of printing, over 800 million iOS devices have been sold and there are over a million apps in the App Store, of which at least 475,000 are native to the iPad. Overall there have been more than 85 billion downloads (all iOS apps).

Beware

With so many apps available, it is difficult to find new apps easily.

184

Hot tip

Even if you delete a previously-purchased app from your iPad you can download it again for free by tapping the **Purchased** tab at the bottom of the App Store screen. Apple will not charge you again for the app.

What are the most popular apps?

These are Books, Games, Entertainment, Education and Utilities.

- Tap **Featured** at the bottom of the screen – if it doesn't show, you may not be on the first App Store screen (tap the back arrow icon to navigate to the first screen)

- Tap **Top Charts** to see the latest apps

- Tap **Explore** to see suggestions based on your current geographical location

- Tap **Purchased** to see previously-purchased apps

- Tap **Updates** to update your apps

Featured Apps

The **Featured** section displays new and recommended apps. This changes frequently so there will be a lot of new apps appearing here on a regular basis. Swipe up and down to view the available content in the Featured section.

Within the **Featured** section are various categories that can help you further refine your app search: Tap on the **See All** link to the right-hand side of each category to see more.

Best New Apps
This shows the apps deemed to be the best new ones in the Store.

Best New Games
This is a selection of the most popular new games apps.

Previews
This is a selection of video previews of various apps that have been selected by the App Store team.

Best New Game Updates
Since games are one of the most popular items in the App Store, there is a category for updates to existing games.

Kids Apps & Games
A selection aimed specifically at children.

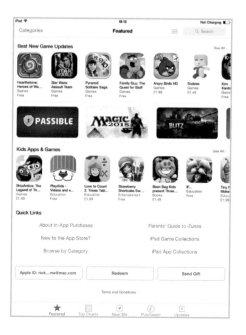

Top Charts

These apps are the most popular. The screen shows the **Top Paid** and **Top Grossing** apps on the left-hand side and the **Free** apps are on the right-hand side.

Categories

There are currently 24 categories of apps in the App Store. This helps (slightly) to find what you're looking for but with more than one million apps, finding an app can be quite difficult! For example, if you tap Lifestyle, you will see more than 2000 apps.

Searching Categories

Within **Top Charts,** tap on the **Categories** button to view the categories from there.

There are magazines and books listing and reviewing apps. Consider investing in one of these to help you find useful apps.

Swipe down to see the full list of categories.

Tap on a category to view the items within it.

Explore

This is a feature which suggests a range of possible apps, some based on your geographic location. To use this:

 Tap on the **Explore** button on the toolbar at the bottom of the App Store

 Tap on the **Allow** button to enable the App Store to use your location (**Location Services** has to be turned On)

Allow "App Store" to access your location while you use the app?
Your location is used to find relevant apps nearby.

Don't Allow   Allow

To turn on Location Services for the App Store, go to **Settings > Privacy > Location Services** and tap on the **App Store** button. Under **Allow Location Access** tap on the **While Using the App** option.

Recommendations will appear in the **Explore** window, with category options in the left-hand panel

Tap on one of the categories to view specific apps for these

In the top of the Explore window is a **Popular Near Me** section that highlights apps that are relevant to your location.

Finding Apps

Standard search methods include

- Knowing what you want! Use the search box.

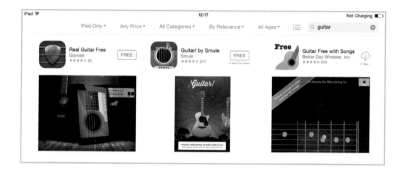

- Knowing roughly where your app is – browse by category.

- Browsing using iTunes on Mac or PC. Check the App Store pane to find what you want. You can download on the computer and transfer to the iPad later.

Use an iPad magazine such as *The Independent Guide to the iPad*, *iPhone Life* among many others. Try browsing websites listing apps such as **appsafari**, **appcraver**, **appshopper**, **148apps**, **ipad-application-reviews.com**, **macworld.com/appguide**, **appspace.com**

Buying Apps

When you identify an app that you would like to use, it can be downloaded to your iPad. To do this:

Don't forget

Apps usually download in a few minutes, or less, depending on the speed of your Wi-Fi connection.

Beware

Some apps have 'in-app purchases'. This is additional content that has to be paid for when it is downloaded.

1 Find the app you want to download and tap on the button next to the app (this will say Free or will have a price)

YouTube
Google, Inc.
★★★☆☆ (813)

FREE

2 The button changes to show **Install**. Tap on this

INSTALL

3 Enter your Apple ID details and tap on the **OK** button

Sign In to iTunes Store
Enter the Apple ID password for "nickvandome@mac.com".

••••••••

Cancel   OK

4 The app will begin to download on your iPad

YouTube
Google, Inc.
★★★☆☆ (813)

5 Once the app is downloaded tap on it to open and use it

Dropbox   YouTube

Safari   Music

Keeping Apps Up-To-Date

App publishers regularly update their software, ironing out bugs and making improvements. The App Store makes it very easy to see if there are any updates for the apps you have downloaded.

How to determine whether updates are available

- You should see a red badge at the top right of the App Store app icon. The number in the circle tells you how many updates you have waiting to be downloaded

- If you don't see a badge there may still be updates available. Open the **App Store** app, tap **Updates** and if there are any these will be listed.
  If none is available then you will see **All Apps Are Up To Date**

- You can update one at a time or all at once

- You will be asked for your iTunes password

- Once entered, the app updates will download in the background

Hot tip

Apps can be set to install updates automatically, from within **Settings > iTunes & App Store** and drag the **Updates** button to **On** under **Automatic Downloads**.

Submitting Reviews

Reviews are useful since they may help you decide whether to buy an app or not.

You can submit reviews for any apps you have downloaded (free or paid).

You *cannot* review any app you do not own.

When you are viewing apps you can read their reviews by tapping on the **Reviews** tab, next to the description of the app.

1 Tap the **App Store** icon to launch the app

2 Find the app you want to review

3 At the top of the screen you should see **Tap a Star to Rate**

You have to download an app before you can review it.

4 Tap on the stars to rate the app between one-five stars (you cannot give any app a zero-star rating)

Even if an app is total rubbish you cannot give it zero stars!

5 Tap in the main **Write a Review** section

6 Enter your text

7 Tap **Send**

8 You can amend the star rating before you hit the Send button

Deleting Apps

There are several ways you can remove apps from the iPad

- Directly using the iPad itself
- Choosing *not* to sync an app using iTunes on your computer

Deleting directly from the iPad

Preinstalled apps (see page 24) cannot be deleted.

1 Press and hold an app's icon until all the icons start jiggling

2 Tap the **X** on the top left corner of the app

3 A box will pop up warning you that you are about to delete an app and all of its data

4 If you still want to delete the app press **Delete**

If you delete an app in the iPad it will remain on your computer.

5 Press the **Home Button** again to stop the apps jiggling

The app has gone from the iPad but is still on your computer.

You can resync the app back to the iPad later if you decide you would like to reinstall it back onto the iPad.

Delete from within iTunes

1 Connect the iPad to your computer

2 Open **iTunes > Apps**

3 You will see your iPad screen shown in the right panel of the iTunes Apps pane

4 Find the app you want to delete and hover your pointer over it until an **X** appears at the top left of the app's icon

5 Click the **X** to delete the app

iTunes U

Although not strictly part of the App Store the iTunes U app can be downloaded from here and used as a great educational resource. iTunes U is a distribution system for lectures, language lessons, films, audiobooks, and lots of other educational content.

Finding educational material on iTunesU

Universities & Colleges	Search for content by educational institution (not every university is listed at present)
Beyond Campus	Other agencies offering educational material for download
K–12	Content for Primary and Secondary education.

Using iTunes U

Finding content in iTunes U is very similar to using the App Store: iTunes U has a **Features** and **Top Charts** section. Tap on the **Subscribe** button when you find a suitable course.

Organizing Apps

When you start downloading apps you will probably soon find that you have dozens, if not hundreds, of them. You can move between screens to view all of your apps by swiping left or right with one finger.

To move an app between screens, tap and hold on it until it starts to jiggle and a cross appears in the corner. Then drag it to the side of the screen. If there is space on the next screen the app will be moved there.

As more apps are added it can become hard to find the apps you want, particularly if you have to swipe between several screens. However, it is possible to organize apps into individual folders to make using them more manageable.
To do this:

1 Press on an app until it starts to jiggle and a white cross appears at the top-left corner

2 Drag the app over another one

...cont'd

Beware

Only top-level folders can be created, i.e. sub-folders cannot be created. Also, one folder cannot be placed within another.

Hot tip

If you want to rename an apps folder after it has been created, tap and hold on it until it starts to jiggle. Then tap on it once and edit the folder name as in Step 5.

 A folder is created, containing the two apps

 The folder is given a default name, usually based on the category of the apps

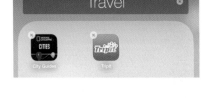

5 Tap on the folder name and type a new name if required

6 Click the **Home Button** once to finish creating the folder

7 Click the **Home Button** again to return to the Home screen (this is done whenever you want to return to the Home screen from an apps folder)

8 The folder is added on the Home screen. Tap on this to access the items within it

16 iBooks

iBooks is an elegant app which lets you browse the iBookstore and save books and PDFs on your bookshelf for reading later. You can read, highlight, use the dictionary, change the appearance of the books and much more.

The iBooks Interface

The iPad is ideal for reading electronic documents including books, and this is a key feature for many people buying the iPad. Just as Apple have made it simple to buy music and other digital content for the iPad, they have done the same with electronic books – ebooks. Browsing and purchasing is simplicity itself. Previewing books before you buy is also possible which saves you buying books you don't want.

The iBooks app provides you with an online **Store** and also a **My Books** section to store books you have purchased or loaded yourself.

A PDF is a document created in the Portable Document Format. This is a versatile format that can be opened and read on a variety of devices. You need to have some form of Adobe Acrobat Reader (or equivalent) functionality on your device to read PDFs.

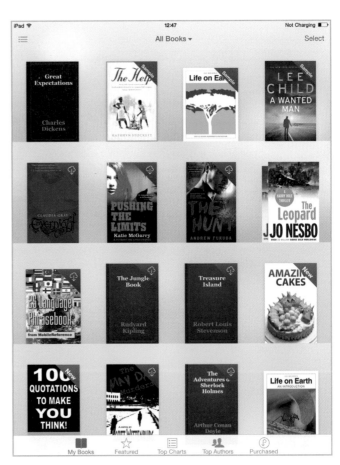

The My Books bookshelf

- You can rearrange the books in the Library by tapping **Edit** and then tapping on books to select them

- **Move** a book to your chosen position by holding on it and dragging it to a new position

- **Delete** books by tapping on the **Delete** button and tapping **Delete This Copy** or **Delete From All Devices**

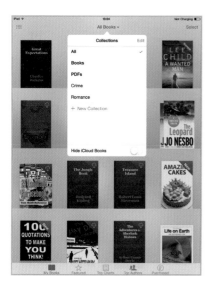

Left: you can browse your collections to see Books, PDFs, etc.

Bottom left: I have tapped **Edit** then tapped one book which I want to delete. I could tap **Delete** and the book would be removed but I've realized I've selected the wrong one!

Below right: after tapping edit I touched one book then dragged it to another shelf.

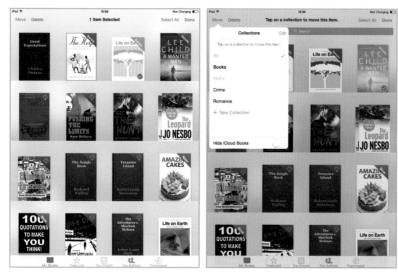

Open a Book

Books (ebooks and PDFs) are stored on shelves in your Library. Just like a real library, you can browse your collection, open and read books, add placeholders, and more.

1 Tap **iBooks**

2 Tap **Library** if iBooks opens on the Store page

3 **Select a book** to read – tap to open

4 Choose a specific point to start reading by sliding your finger along the thumbnails at the bottom. The current page is shown as a slightly larger thumbnail

If you close the app or book, iBooks will remember the place and the next time you open it the book will be opened at the same page as you left it.

Flicking through a book

 Tap **iBooks** to open it and **Choose a book** to read

 Move through the pages by **tapping right or left margins** (moves you forward and backwards through the book). Or you can **touch and hold the bottom corner** moving your finger towards the top left

 To move to the previous page, touch and hold the left margin and slide your finger L → R across the screen

To move to a specific page in a book

 Tap the **page** in the center. Controls will appear on the screen

 Drag the **navigator** at the bottom of the screen to the page you want

Viewing the Table of Contents

 Tap the page near the center, Controls should appear

 Tap **Contents**

Add a bookmark to a book
This helps you find your place in a book (you can add multiple bookmarks).

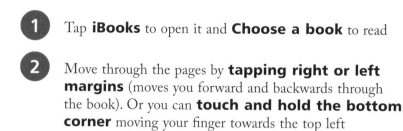 While the book is open, touch a word in the top right-hand corner

> Great Expectations   ₐA   Q   ▌
>
> ## Chapter X
>
> ─⊗⊗⊗─
>
> ea occurred to me a morning or two later

Remove the bookmark later by tapping on the red bookmark icon

Hot tip

Add as many bookmarks as you want to your book – and remove them just as easily!

...cont'd

Want the book read to you?
You will need to activate VoiceOver
(**Settings > Accessibility > VoiceOver**).

Highlighting text
You can use highlighters on a physical book to mark specific pieces of text. The same can be done using an ebook.

Hot tip

The iPad can read books to you (not PDFs, though).

1 Open the page of a book

2 Press and hold your finger on a word within the text that you want to highlight

3 Drag the **anchor points** to include the text

4 Choose **highlight** from the pop-up menu. Your selected text will now have a yellow highlight applied

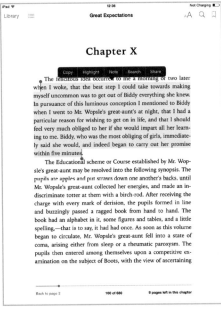

5 To remove the highlights, tap the **text** again and then select **Remove Highlight**

To select an entire paragraph
Tap anywhere in the paragraph with two fingers. The whole paragraph will be selected.

Using the Dictionary

The in-built dictionary is instantly accessible within your books (but not PDF files).

 Open the page of a book and tap and hold the **word** you want to look up in the dictionary

 Tap **Define**

 The phonetic pronunciation and definitions will appear in a pop-up box

 Tap the page to **close** the dictionary

Hot tip

The Dictionary is not available when reading a PDF.

---

iPad 🔋 12:36 Not Charging

Library

Great Expectations AA 🔍 🔖

‹ Dictionary **felicitous**

felicitous | fə'lisətəs |
adjective

well chosen or suited to the circumstances: a felicitous phrase.

• pleasing and fortunate: the view was the room's only felicitous feature.

DERIVATIVES

felicitously adverb .

Manage Search Web

The felicitous ... o later when I woke, that ... naking myself uncommon w ... knew. In pursuance of this ... Biddy when I went to Mr. ... had a particular reason for ... should feel very much oblig ... learning to me. Biddy, wh ... ediately said she would, and indeed began to carry out her promise within five minutes.

The Educational scheme or Course established by Mr. Wopsle's great-aunt may be resolved into the following synopsis. The pupils ate apples and put straws down one another's backs, until Mr. Wopsle's great-aunt collected her energies, and made an indiscriminate totter at them with a birch-rod. After receiving the charge with every mark of derision, the pupils formed in line and buzzingly passed a ragged book from hand to hand. The book had an alphabet in it, some figures and tables, and a little spelling,—that is to say, it had had once. As soon as this volume began to circulate, Mr. Wopsle's great-aunt fell into a state of coma, arising either from sleep or a rheumatic paroxysm. The pupils then entered among themselves upon a competitive examination on the subject of Boots, with the view of ascertaining

Back to page 2 100 of 680 9 pages left in this chapter

Find Occurrences of Words

You can search an entire book or document for the occurrence of a specific word.

 Open the page of a book

 Tap and hold the **word** for which you want to find occurrences

 Tap **Search**

4 Enter the word you wish to search for

A dropdown list of all pages containing that word will appear.

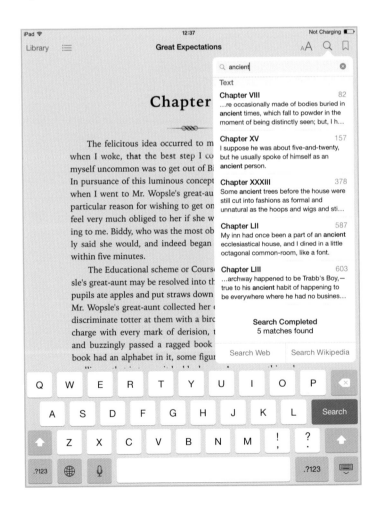

Adjust the Screen Brightness

Depending on the ambient lighting you may need to adjust the screen brightness. For example, if you read in a dark room you could turn the brightness down, whereas outside in sunshine you might need to turn the brightness up.

 With the page of a book open, tap **settings**

2 Tap and hold the **slider** to adjust the brightness

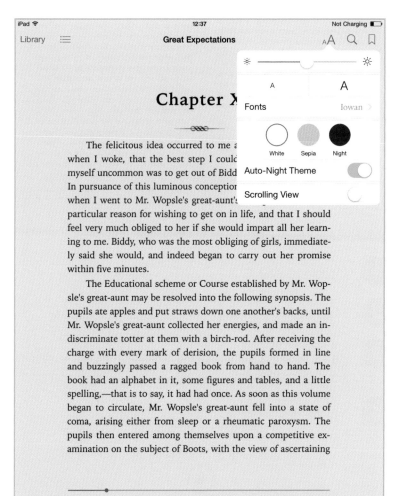

Portrait or Landscape?

The iPad adjusts the orientation of the page depending on how you hold it. If you turn it sideways the pages rotate. This is not particularly convenient when you are lying down.

To avoid automatic rotation of the book pages

 Open a book

 Hold the iPad in either portrait or landscape mode

 Swipe up from the bottom of the screen to access the Control Center

 Tap on this button so it appears locked

Reading a book is one of the times when it is definitely useful to lock the screen, especially if you are lying down!

Using the iBookstore

This is a great resource containing many of the popular titles, with more being added daily. The iBookstore is like iTunes except you buy books rather than music, and there is no rental option. Browsing the iBookstore requires an active Internet connection.

Purchased list

This view shows all the books you have purchased (including those titles which are free).

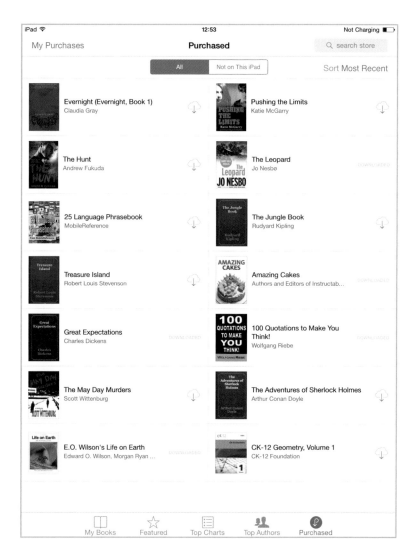

Beware

You need an iTunes account even if you want to download free books.

...cont'd

Browsing is made incredibly easy. You can browse by category or search for specific items.

You can search books by

- **Featured**
- **Top Charts**
- **Top Authors**
- **Categories**
- Typing your **search** terms into the search box

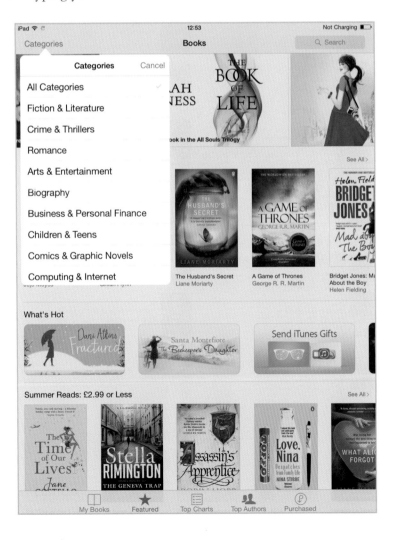

Sample chapters

You can't download music samples in iTunes although you can hear 30-second audio samples before you buy, but you *are* allowed to download short sample chapters of books before you commit to buy. If you like the sample you will probably go back and buy the full title.

Downloading sample chapters

1 Open **iBooks** and find a book that you are interested in

2 Tap the book cover to bring up the information window which floats on top of the current page

3 Tap the **Sample** button and this will be downloaded to your library. This will usually be one or two chapters of the title

4 Tap the sample in your iBooks Library to open it and start reading

Changing Fonts and Size

Sometimes the font or its size makes it difficult to read a book. With a physical book you cannot change the font but with ebooks you can control the typeface and its size, to make the book as readable as possible.

To change the font or font size

1 Open a book in iBooks

2 Decide which orientation you will use to read the book – portrait or landscape

3 Tap the **font icon**

4 Tap small or large **A** to make font smaller or larger

5 To change the font itself tap **Fonts**

6 Choose from the dropdown list

7 The book pages may have a light brown tint (**sepia effect**). If you like this, keep Sepia **ON**. If you want clinically white pages turn Sepia **OFF**

Hot tip

Font too small? Don't like the typeface? Change it!

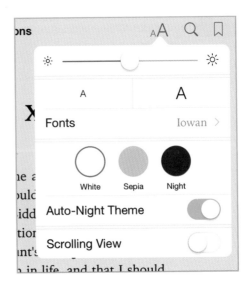

Purchasing Books

Providing you have an iTunes account you can download paid or free books from the iBookstore.

1 Open **iBooks**

2 Tap **Store** if you are currently in Library mode

3 Find a book you want to buy

4 Tap its icon to bring up the floating window showing the price

5 Tap the **gray price box**. This will turn green and will say **Buy Book**

6 Tap **Buy Book** (if the book is free it will say **Get Book** instead)

Cop Town
Karin Slaughter
Published: 28 May 2014
Print Length: 416 Pages
No Ratings

BUY BOOK   SAMPLE

Details   Reviews   Related

Book Description

'Karin Slaughter is simply one of the best thriller writers working today, and Cop Town shows the author at the top of her game – relentless pacing, complex characters, and gritty realism, all set against the backdrop of a city on the edge. Slaughter's eye for detail and truth is unmatched . . . I'd follow her anywhere.' Gillian Flynn, author of Gone Girl
...more

Information

Language   English
Category   Fiction & Literature
Publisher   Random House
Seller   The Random House Group Ltd.
Published   28 May 2014
Size   2.9 MB
Print Length   416 Pages

Requirements

To view this book, you must have an iOS device with iBooks 1.3.1 or later and iOS 4.3.3 or later, or a Mac with iBooks 1.0 or later and OS X 10.9 or later.

7 The book will begin to download into your library and the view will change from Store → Library. You will be prompted for your **Apple ID password**

8 Once entered, the book will download

Find More Books by Author

If you have a favorite author or you just want to find more books by the same author you can.

 Tap the **book cover** to bring up the Information screen with a range of details about the book

 Tap the **Related** button

 You will then see any other books on the iBook Store by the same author

Hot tip

Setting up iBooks alerts is not obvious. To set up alerts go to **Settings > iTunes & App Store** then tap **Apple ID**. Then tap **View Apple ID**. Sign in with your password and scroll down to **My Alerts**. Set up your alerts from the options shown.

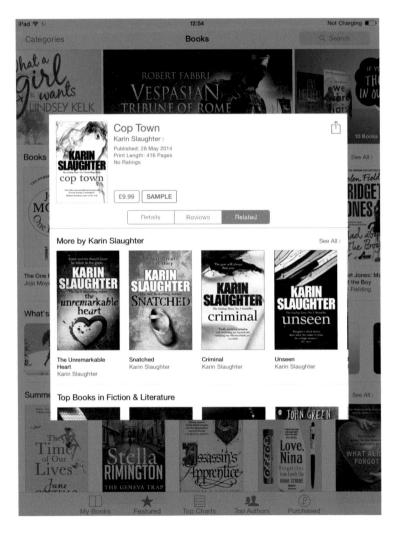

Tell A Friend

You can let other people know about books by sending links to books which they can view on their computer.

 Tap on a book title to view its details

 Tap the **Share** icon

Select one of the sharing options including messaging, emailing or sharing via a social networking site

If you see something great – share with a friend. It's very easy to do.

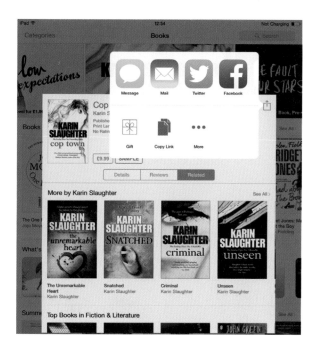

4 Depending on the selection in Step 3, information about the item is displayed for the required person, who can then view the item in the iBooks Store, if desired

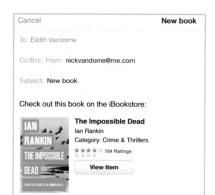

eBooks From Other Sources

You are not completely limited to iBookstore for your electronic books for the iPad.

ePub books

 Download an ePub book (**epubbooks.com**)

 Add to iTunes (drag and drop the book straight onto iTunes)

3 Connect iPad and sync ePub books to iPad

Other sources for ebooks

- Smashwords (**smashwords.com**)

- Google Books (**books.google.com**)

- Kindle iPad app (**amazon.com**)

- Design your own – many programs allow you to export your files in ePub format, e.g. Adobe InDesign, Storyist, Sigil, and others. Whatever software you use, if it can be saved in the ePub format you can get it onto the iPad. Another option is to save your work as a PDF but you cannot search PDFs for words, or use the dictionary. But it does let you read the document easily

The iBookstore is not the only source of ebooks for the iPad. Most books in epub format will work with the iPad.

17 The iPad at Work

Sadly, work gets in the way of all this play but the iPad makes giving presentations, writing documents and number-crunching fun! Instead of dragging a heavy laptop to your next meeting, try taking your iPad instead. There's not much you can't do with it!

Storing, Syncing and Editing

The iPad is different to a conventional computer or laptop. There is no "desktop" which means you cannot drag and drop files around and place them in folders, like you would with your laptop.

However, there are still ways of copying files to and from your iPad, allowing you to read and edit text documents, spreadsheets and presentations, and copy them back to your Mac or PC.

There are several apps available that allow you to get files onto the iPad including:

Dropbox (dropbox.com)	Popular on Mac and PC. Provides cloud storage which you can access from any computer. The free account gives you 2GB storage
Documents To Go and Quickoffice	Documents To Go and Quickoffice essentially do the same thing – they let you read and edit Microsoft Office files. They let you keep local (iPad) and remote (on your PC or Mac) files
iCloud	iCloud gives you 5GB free storage. The downside is, it isn't a folder where you can drag and drop your files. Useful for keeping things in sync though
Evernote	Useful for storing clippings, web pages, PDFs, Word files and others. The free account provides 2GB storage and file types are restricted (images, audio, PDF and web pages)

Configure the iPad to view documents

With your iPad connected to your computer, click the **Apps** tab in iTunes. At the bottom of the screen you will see an option for **File Sharing**.

You can configure apps on the iPad to open documents on your iPad. Once you click an app, e.g. Documents To Go, a list of files readable by Documents To Go will appear. Click to select all those you want Documents To Go to open. Then click **Add...**

Hot tip

Dropbox is very useful for storing files and is available for PC, Mac, iPad, iPhone and iPod Touch (for more information see page 227). But if you want to edit the files you will need additional software such as Documents To Go or similar. Check out the App Store.

How you edit your document depends on what app you use on the iPad.

Editing Word documents using Documents To Go

1. Open **Documents To Go** on the iPad

2. Navigate to **Desktop** to add a file from your computer

3. Choose the computer you want to connect to. Tap **My Documents To Go** to see folder contents on the computer

4. Tap the **file** you want to edit (and save locally on the iPad)

5. Once open, tap **Save As**

6. Tap **Location** to navigate back to the local storage, i.e. iPad

7. Tap **Local Files**

8. Tap **Select**

9. Tap **Save**

You can now edit and save the file. In PowerPoint you can add notes and edit your slides (in Outline mode only).

Hot tip

Word files can be read and edited easily on the iPad.

Apple iWork Suite

Apple designed a suite of apps called iWork which includes a word processor (**Pages**), spreadsheet (**Numbers**), and presentation package (**Keynote**). The suite has many functions similar to Microsoft Office. All three apps are available as free downloads from the App Store (for compatible iOS 8 devices).

Hot tip

Apple's iWork suite is available for the iPad and is very close to the computer version.

Beware

If you use Dropbox to store your word processing documents you will find that although you can open them in Pages you cannot save the changed document back to Dropbox. Annoying? However, for $5 a month you can open a DropDAV account and open and save back to Dropbox. Very easy to set up.

Pages

1 Tap **Pages** to open

2 Select a **Document** by flicking through the list from L → R

3 Or create a new document with the **+** button

4 Select from the choice of **Templates**

5 **Edit** the text

6 Add **graphics** and then tap media – choose illustrations

7 When finished, tap **Documents** and the document will be saved

8 To **rename** tap the name and enter your own title

9 Tap **Done**

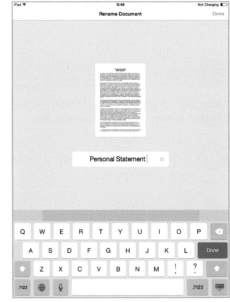

Share documents by tapping the share icon then email, print, copy to iTunes or WebDAV.

Pages will happily open documents created in Microsoft Word and other formats, and can export in several formats including Microsoft Word.

Pages will import Microsoft Word files easily, though some formatting may be lost.

Pages shows you a window containing all documents in the Pages "folder". Flick up or down until you find what you want.

...cont'd

Keynote

Keynote is Apple's presentation app. It is similar to PowerPoint, although cropping and adding shapes is a bit different. Some aspects of slide design, such as cropping images and creation of shapes, is undoubtedly easier using a mouse but simple slides can be created using the iPad.

Open an existing presentation

1 Tap **Keynote** to open the app

2 Unlike Pages, Keynote only uses landscape mode

3 Flick L → R through existing presentations

4 Find the one you want and tap to open

5 You will see thumbnails down the left side with the slides occupying the rest of the screen

To create a new presentation

1 Tap the **+** button and tap on **Create Presentation**

2 Choose a **Template**

3 Tap **+** to add a new slide – a panel showing available Master slides will appear. Select the one that suits your content

4 Add your text

5 **Save** by tapping **Presentations**

6 **Name** the presentation by tapping its name and entering your own title

7 Save to iTunes or leave on the iPad

Hot tip

Creating new presentations using Keynote on the iPad is cumbersome and I would strongly recommend you create your presentations using a Mac. You can edit these on the iPad later if necessary.

If you save your iWork files (including Keynote) to iCloud you will have ready access from your Mac or iOS device.

Keynote can open PowerPoint files.

Like Pages, Keynote will open Microsoft PowerPoint files. The presentation above was created in PowerPoint and saved before opening in Keynote. Flick right or left to see what presentations are available.

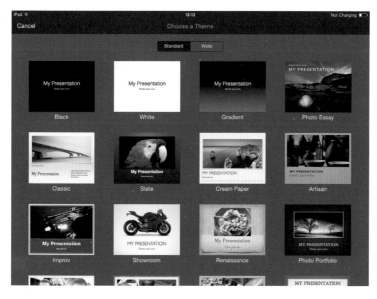

The iPad version of Keynote looks almost identical to the desktop version. Note the thumbnails down the left margin with the current (highlighted) slide showing in the main screen.

...cont'd

Numbers

Numbers is similar to Microsoft Excel. Data is entered in tabular form and can be used to create all types of charts. Numbers can be used in portrait and landscape modes.

1 Tap **Numbers** to open the app

2 **Enter data** into spreadsheet

3 Make sure you have selected the correct data type for your columns (**42** = numeric, **◯** = date/time, **T** = text, **⊟** = calculation)

4 Create **chart**

5 **Save** by tapping **Spreadsheets**

6 **Rename** by tapping its name

7 **Save** to iTunes or elsewhere

Using iPad for Presentations

Just as you would use your laptop to present your PowerPoint or Keynote slides, you can use your iPad once you hook it up to an AV projector or screen.

You will need to buy the Lightning to VGA Adapter. This plugs into the bottom of the iPad and the other end connects to the VGA projector.

Present using an AV projector

1 **Connect** the iPad to the projector using the Lightning to VGA Adapter

The iPad is great for giving presentations and saves you having to drag a heavy laptop around!

If you have access to an HD display you would be better using the HDMI connector (Lightning Digital AV Adapter).

2 Open **Keynote**

3 Choose **Presentation**

The file will open in Presentation mode (rather than Edit mode).

Editing Microsoft Office Files

You have a number of options, such as Documents To Go, Quickoffice, and a number of other apps to edit Microsoft Office files.

1 **Connect** the iPad to your computer

2 In iTunes go to **Apps tab** and scroll down to File Sharing

3 Click the **app** you want to use to edit your Office files

4 Click the **files** on the right to add them to the iPad

5 Open the **app** you want to use on the iPad, e.g. Documents To Go

6 Go to **Local** to see the files on the iPad

7 Locate document and tap to open OR if you want to open in another app, tap the arrow and choose **Open in...** and select the app from the dropdown list

This document has been opened in Pages, but could just as easily have been opened in Documents To Go natively.

Here is the same document opened in GoodReader, Documents To Go and Quickoffice.

In this example, the document has been opened in Documents To Go. The text is perfectly readable, and can be edited, copied and pasted.

Here the document has been opened in GoodReader (a PDF-type app like Adobe Acrobat Reader). The text can be read, copied but not edited.

Here we have used the iPhone version of Quickoffice. The iPhone version runs just fine but the size is not optimized for the iPad screen. In order to try to fill the screen the picture has to be doubled in size, resulting in pixilation of the text.

There is version for iPad called Quickoffice Pro HD.

Get the Latest News

Because the iPad is such a great ebook reader, lots of publishers have made their content available for the Web and iPad. This includes newspapers and journals. Many offer free registration, while others have limited content, with a paid subscription for full content. They are available through the Newsstand app.

Hot tip

The iPad is great for reading newspapers, journals, and magazines.

Keep up with politics and economic news.

A range of lifestyle magazines.

Magazines for a wide variety of hobbies.

For the latest in Mac news you can subscribe to Macworld and several other Mac magazines.

Organization Apps

In the App Store there is a wide range of organization apps for tasks such as note-taking. Some of these are:

- **Evernote.** As mentioned on page 216, this is one of the most popular note-taking apps. You can create individual notes and also save them into notebook folders. Evernote works across multiple devices so, if it is installed on other computers or mobile devices, you can access your notes wherever you are.

- **Popplet.** This is a note-taking app that enables you to link notes together, so you can form a mindmap-type creation. You can also include photos and draw pictures.

- **Dropbox.** This is an online service for storing and accessing files. You can upload files from your iPad and then access them from other devices with an Internet connection.

- **Bamboo Paper.** This is another note-taking app, but it allows you to do this by handwriting rather than typing. The free version comes with one notebook into which you can put your notes and the paid-for version provides another 20.

- **Errands To-Do List.** A virtual To-Do list that can help keep you organized and up-to-date. You can create your own folders for different items and have alerts remind you of important dates, events and items.

- **Notability.** Another app that utilizes handwriting for creating notes. It also accommodates word processing, and audio recording.

- **Alarmed.** An app for keeping you on time and up-to-date. It has an alarm clock, pop-up reminders and pop-up timers.

- **Grocery List.** Shopping need never be the same again with this virtual shopping list app.

- **World Calendar.** Find out public holiday information for 40 countries around the world.

Printing from iPad

The iPad can now support direct printing (called **AirPrint**).

Hot tip

Good news! You can print directly from the iPad. If Apple's in-built options don't work there are third-party apps which will make printing easy.

iPad 🛜	14:00	❊ 5% ▭

‹ Inbox (3)   ∧ ∨   🏳 🗁 🗑 ↩ ✎

From: Andrew Mitchell ›   Reply

To: Andrew Mitchell ›   Reply All

Perth Concert - Civic Reception Invitation - RSVP   Forward
18 August 2013 12:23

Hi All,   Print

Apple has provided support for many printers, and a full list can be found at **http://support.apple.com/kb/HT4356**

Available apps that enable iPad printing

- PrintCentral
- PrinterShare
- ePrint
- DocPrinter
- ActivePrint
- Print n Share

Print web page using Print n Share

1 Copy the web page URL to the clipboard

2 Open Print n Share and select **Web pages** from the options at the bottom of the screen

3 Paste URL into box at the top then tap the printer icon

4 Print from screen or from the actual web URL (the latter is probably better)

5 Choose your printer by tapping **Choose**

6 Tap **Print**

18 Accessibility Options

The iPad has some very effective adjustments which make it easy to use for people with visual and other impairments. This chapter highlights the main accessibility settings which will make the iPad work for you even if you have sight or auditory issues.

Universal Access

Similar to the iPhone, the iPad has a variety of settings that make it easier for people with visual and hearing problems to use.

- Universal Access features

- Playback of Closed Captions

- VoiceOver screen reader

- Full-screen magnification

- White on Black

- Mono audio

Not all features are available for every app. Zoom, White on Black, and Mono Audio work with all apps, but VoiceOver only works with the in-built apps and some apps on the App Store.

Use iTunes to turn Accessibility On and Off

1 Connect your iPad to the computer

2 Within iTunes select **iPad** in the sidebar

3 Click on the **Summary** pane

4 Click **Configure Accessibility,** under **Options**

5 Select the **features** you want to use

VoiceOver

This setting enables the iPad to tell you what's on the screen even if you cannot see the screen.

 Touch the screen or drag your fingers to hear the screen items described

 If text is selected, VoiceOver will read the text to you

To turn VoiceOver On

 Go to **Settings > General > Accessibility > VoiceOver**

 Tap **VoiceOver** to turn On or Off

 Tap **Speak Hints** On or Off

If you cannot see the screen text, VoiceOver will read it to you.

VoiceOver gestures

Tap	Speak item
Flick Right or Left	Select next or previous item
Flick Up or Down	Depends on Rotor Control setting
Two-finger tap	Stop speaking current selection
Two-finger flick Up	Read all from top of screen
Two-finger flick Down	Read all from current position
Three-finger flick Up/Down	Scroll one page at a time
Three-finger flick Right/Left	Next or previous page
Three-finger tap	Speak the scroll status
Four-finger flick Up/Down	Go to first or last element on page
Four-finger flick Right/Left	Next or previous section

Accessibility Features

There are numerous other accessibility features that can be deployed on the iPad. These can all be accessed from **Settings > General > Accessibility**:

Vision
The Vision options include the following:

- **VoiceOver**. (see page 231).

- **Zoom**. This can be used to increase and decrease the screen magnification. Double-tap the screen with three fingers to increase the magnification by 200%. Double-tap with three fingers again to reduce the magnification. Drag with three fingers to move around the screen.

- **Invert Colors**. This setting completely inverts the iPad colors, from white on black to black on white.

- **Speak Selection.** This can be used to speak out selected text. Tap on the Speak button that appears.

- **Speak Auto-text**. Turning on this option lets the iPad speak the text corrections as you type.

< General	Accessibility	
VISION		
VoiceOver		Off >
Zoom		Off >
Invert Colors		
Grayscale		
Speech		>
Larger Text		Off >
Bold Text		
Button Shapes		
Increase Contrast		>
Reduce Motion		Off >
On/Off Labels		

- **Larger Type**. Use this to allow compatible apps to increase the size of text.

- **Bold Text**. This can be turned on to create bold text on the iPad. It requires a restart to apply it.

- **Increase Contrast**. This aids legibility by increasing the contrast with some backgrounds.

- **Reduce Motion**. This reduces the amount of motion effects that are applied throughout the iPad.

- **On/Off Labels**. This defines the On/Off buttons further by adding labels to them as well as their standard colors.

Hearing

The Hearing options include the following:

- **Subtitles & Captioning**. This determines the style of captions on the iPad, if used.

- **Mono Audio**. Instead of stereo sound, the Mono Audio channels both right and left output into a single mono output. This is useful for people with hearing impairment, since they can hear the output from both channels in one ear. Turn Mono Audio On and Off.

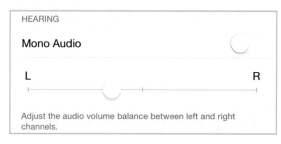

Learning

The Learning options are:

- **Guided Access**. The Guided Access option allows for certain functionality within an app to be disabled so that individual tasks can be focused on without any other distractions. For instance, areas of a web page can be disabled so that the page being viewed cannot be moved away from.

...cont'd

Interaction

The Interaction options include the following:

- **Switch Control**. This can be used to set up your iPad for an adaptive accessory such as a mouse, keyboard or joy stick.

- **Assistive Touch**. This contains a range of options that reduce the need for using your hands and fingers as much as for standard use.

INTERACTION	
Switch Control	Off >
AssistiveTouch	Off >
Home-click Speed	Default >

- **Home-click Speed**. This can be used to adjust the speed for double-clicking and triple-clicking the Home button.

Accessibility Shortcuts

These are settings for selecting options for the functions that are activated by triple-clicking the Home button.

‹ Accessibility **Accessibility Shortcut**
TRIPLE-CLICK THE HOME BUTTON FOR:
Guided Access ✓
VoiceOver
Invert Colors
Grayscale
Zoom
Switch Control
AssistiveTouch

Index

T

U

V

W

Z